THE FACTS ABOUT CAESAREAN BIRTHS

Did you know:

• Any woman about to give birth faces a one in four chance of having her baby delivered by caesarean section.

• If you deliver by c-section, you can deliver vaginally in subsequent pregnancies, with certain exceptions.

• Studies show that a major determinant of whether a woman will have a caesarean is the "c-rate" of her doctor.

• Blood loss with a caesarean is about two times that of normal delivery.

Protect yourself against unnecessary surgery. Be fully informed if circumstances *do* warrant surgical birth. You'll find everything you need to know to make a wise, informed decision in . . .

THE WELL-INFORMED PATIENT'S GUIDE TO CAESAREAN BIRTHS

THE DELL SURGICAL LIBRARY:

THE WELL-INFORMED PATIENT'S GUIDE TO
   HYSTERECTOMY

THE WELL-INFORMED PATIENT'S GUIDE TO
   CORONARY BYPASS SURGERY

THE WELL-INFORMED PATIENT'S GUIDE TO
   CAESAREAN BIRTHS

THE WELL-INFORMED PATIENT'S GUIDE TO
   CATARACT AND OTHER EYE SURGERY

DELL SURGICAL LIBRARY

THE WELL-INFORMED PATIENT'S GUIDE TO

CAESAREAN BIRTHS

KATHRYN COX, M.D., AND JUDITH D. SCHWARTZ

A DELL BOOK

Published by
Dell Publishing
a division of
Bantam Doubleday Dell Publishing Group, Inc.
666 Fifth Avenue
New York, New York 10103

This book is not intended as a substitute for medical advice of physicians and should be used only in conjunction with the advice of your personal doctor. The reader should regularly consult a physician in matters relating to his or her health and particularly in respect of any symptoms which may require diagnosis or medical attention.

Published by arrangement with G. S. Sharpe Communications, Inc., 606 West 116 Street, New York, New York 10027.

ISBN: 0-440-20712-6

Printed in the United States of America
Published simultaneously in Canada

April 1991

10 9 8 7 6 5 4 3 2 1

OPM

Contents

Be Realistic about Labor
Understand Your Own Feelings about Labor
Stay in Touch with What Your Body Needs
Be Realistic about Medication
Don't Go to the Hospital Too Early
Don't Negatively Affect Labor

List of Figures

Introduction

Saying the very word *caesarean* to a woman planning to give birth is likely to provoke a heated response. Over the last two decades, the rate of caesarean births in the United States has soared. Any woman on the threshold of childbirth now faces a one in four chance of having her baby delivered by abdominal surgery. As recently as 1970, the odds were only one in twenty.

Caesarean births (also called caesarean sections or c-sections) are now the most common surgical procedure that women of childbearing years undergo. As a nation, this represents a tremendous cost in terms of health (the added risk to mothers and infants) as well as economics (the total hospital bill for a caesarean may be double that of a vaginal birth). The staggering caesarean rate is clearly one of the most vexing problems in medicine today. If current trends continue, the annual number of caesareans will soon reach one million.

But many caesareans are necessary, and without them, a significant number of deliveries would be perilous for mother and child. Women with conditions like diabetes and severe hypertension might not even have the option of giving birth at all. Even though a caesarean

mother is hospitalized for an average of five days—
and once she gets home, she still has to recover
from surgery, as well as get used to her new role as
mother—many women regard this discomfort as a price
well worth paying if the reward is a healthy, thriving
baby.

But their sheer frequency is making them routine,
and experts agree that a sizable percentage of caesareans performed today in the United States are medically
unjustified. Caesareans are, in fact, major abdominal
operations, and their risks and their complication rates
are higher than those of vaginal deliveries. Medical
experts and women's health advocates contend that in
many instances, mother and child are better off if nature is given a chance to do more of the work.

The caesarean question has therefore been intensely
debated of late. A woman who learns that she is a
candidate for a caesarean may well feel caught in the
middle of the conflict. She may have heard stories
about women who regard their caesareans as crimes
against them—but also stories from others who had
agonizing, exhausting vaginal births. She may become
fearful about her pregnancy and want to do everything
possible to ensure the health of her baby. She may
suddenly question her doctor's judgment. (This in itself
can be upsetting, since the doctor is the person in
whom she's entrusted her own—and her baby's—health.)
She may have prepared herself psychologically for a
natural childbirth, and she may feel angry that the
possible operation could squelch her and her husband's
plans. In short, she's frightened about the consequences
of having a caesarean—and of the consequences of not
having one. The result is often confusion or rage at
what is already a stressful and emotional time.

If you are in this position, you should keep in mind that it's *your* pregnancy and *your* delivery. A birth isn't something that just happens to you unawares; by playing an active role in making choices about the birth of your child, you can minimize your chances of having an unwarranted caesarean. You can usually plan ahead for the possibility that a caesarean will have to be performed, so that it will be handled as you wish. You can arrange to have your husband present, for example, or to be given a minimum of medication.

You should become informed about the various issues relating to caesareans (including prenatal care and nutrition, medication, and labor techniques) and about the aspects of your own pregnancy that may or may not lead to one. You should find a doctor (or a midwife) who will work well with you. For some women, such as those who have previously had a caesarean but are now planning a vaginal birth, this may not be an easy task, but the result may more than make up for the effort. Find the place that best suits the birth you want. Hospitals vary in atmosphere and attitude, so this too may require some checking around.

Be realistic about your childbirth expectations. Some women actively want caesareans, thinking that it will be easier than going through the long, strenuous process of labor. But here the pain of surgery and the subsequent recovery is merely substituted for the pain of natural labor. Similarly, some women are prepared for the joys of vaginal birth but not for its discomforts; they may be truly stunned by the actual task and indeed feel relief if a caesarean is proposed after a long labor.

Regardless of the means of delivery, a woman who

feels that the birth has been seized from her is likely to feel disappointed, if not devastated. Only by taking control of your own childbirth plans can you ensure that you'll do what's best for you and your baby as well as feel positive about it.

Progress is being made. The year 1987 was the first year in a couple of decades that the caesarean rate didn't rise but remained stable. The American College of Obstetricians and Gynecologists has now adopted the policy that women who have previously had caesareans should be encouraged to attempt a vaginal delivery for their next pregnancy. New York State has instituted a program to reduce the rate of caesarean births. Studies have demonstrated that hospitals have had success with extremely low caesarean rates (notably, North Central Bronx in New York), prompting the medical establishment to rethink its assumptions about caesareans. And a great many caring practitioners and advocates are working toward safer, less intrusive, and more humane childbirth.

Equally important, women are becoming more knowledgeable about their bodies and more assertive in making their demands. They are coming to recognize that they have certain rights—including the right to a humane delivery, the right to be informed about proposed drugs and procedures, and the right to a second opinion before surgery. They have become more active medical consumers and increasingly question traditional attitudes and practices instead of taking things—in this case, literally—lying down. Although the vast majority of women deliver in hospitals, women giving birth are not ill; rather, they're at the peak of their health and deserve to be treated as such.

But there's a long way to go yet. In some hospitals, a

woman still has a 50 percent chance of undergoing a caesarean. Some physicians still prefer to schedule a caesarean rather than take the chance that they will be called in to deliver a baby vaginally at an inopportune time. (These physicians may or may not be conscious that their preference is affecting their decision.) Despite ample documentation confirming that vaginal births after previous caesareans are safe, many physicians still discourage their patients from having them. Research on the long-term effects that certain procedures and medications may have on children has yet to be assembled. And not surprisingly, a great deal of confusion among women persists.

In this book, we aim to clear away some of the confusion surrounding caesareans. We hope to answer most of your questions about the procedure and suggest ways to avoid unnecessary medical intervention and its aftereffects—both to you and your child. This book is neither a defense of caesareans nor a political treatise against them. Rather, it provides straightforward guidance to expectant mothers (and to women who have had caesareans) about the caesarean operation to set them on the path to a rewarding and wonderful birth.

CHAPTER 1

Caesarean Births: The Controversy in Context

Case History: As far as Tracey was concerned, there was no question about it—she was not going to have a caesarean. Never a big fan of doctors or hospitals, she was going to deliver her baby her way. She took childbirth classes and practiced Lamaze. No one, she felt, could be better prepared than she.

Then came her delivery. Tracey was in labor for twenty-eight hours and was pushing actively for two and a half of them. During this excruciating phase, the baby simply failed to descend. She was given epidural anesthesia for the pain. After another half hour, a caesarean was performed. All went smoothly, with no complications to speak of.

But months later, Tracey, a healthy twenty-eight-year-old, still felt completely wiped out and despondent. She hadn't wanted this to happen, but it had. She felt terrible, as if she had let herself, her baby, and everybody else down.

Case History: Cheryl, thirty-two, was in the midst of a difficult labor. Although, to the best of his ability, her doctor had predicted that the delivery would be uncomplicated, progress was very slow, and the baby seemed not to want to move. After a good deal of pushing and shifting of position, the fetal monitor began to register fetal distress. Corrective measures were to no avail. A sample of blood from the baby's scalp confirmed that the situation was serious, and the doctor performed a caesarean to prevent the baby from being harmed.

Cheryl's later response was "I'd hesitate to say that I was thrilled with how it went. But it's all behind me. I have my son now, and I know that I did everything I could have done."

CAESAREANS PRO AND CON

One reason caesareans are controversial today is that both the medical community and the public are beginning to question what has hitherto been a clear trend in this century: increased medical interventions in childbirth. The basic "tools" of midwifery (hot compresses and gentle hands) have given way to a formidible array of medical machinery (monitors, IVs, various forms of anesthesia). Women giving birth have become "patients." Control over labor has passed from the expectant mother (who in the past may have directed the activities of those around her) to the obstetrician. Indeed, even of ordinary births it is said that the doctor "delivered" the baby, even though it could justifiably be said that the mother "delivered" the baby; after all, it was her motions and contractions that moved the baby through the canal and "delivered" the baby into the doctor's waiting hands.

Still, without the caesarean option, a great many births today would end tragically for the mother or for her child or both. In certain emergency situations—such as when a misplacement or separation of the placenta causes hemorrhage or when the umbilical cord is wrapped tightly around the baby's neck—surgery is imperative. Babies in certain breech positions or babies who are quite large are also better off being delivered abdominally. Certain maternal conditions, too, may necessitate surgical intervention, including diabetes, hypertension, and active herpes infection, although in some situations, the advisability of a caesarean has to be determined on an individual basis. Other indications—such as a small pelvis, failed induction, fetal stress, and previous caesarean—are often less clear cut. In many instances, a caesarean may prove the best course for both mother and child. But in other cases, an uncomplicated vaginal delivery may indeed be feasible, given willingness and patience on the part of the mother and her doctor. Whenever possible, a vaginal delivery is preferable because it saves the mother from a significant abdominal operation.

It's beyond argument that the availability of safe caesareans has contributed to the welfare of mothers and their infants. But above a certain rate, caesareans work to the detriment of health because of the risks and side effects inherent in the surgery. Many women also report feeling depressed or that they've "failed" as women after caesareans. While this emotional reaction can be lessened in a number of ways—particularly by anticipating in advance the possibility of a caesarean and preparing for it—it can detract from the joy of child-birth and affect the mother's feelings at a crucial time for bonding with her newborn.

The point is that women need to be informed about what to expect with a caesarean, for the facts are not always presented. They need to work with their physicians so that they choose the mode of delivery best suited to their needs.

UNNECESSARY CAESAREANS

How many caesarean births are unnecessary? That's a difficult question to answer, for second-guessing how a birth would have turned out had the delivery been different can never be accurate. But a number of figures give clues. First is the rate of repeat caesareans. Repeat caesareans now constitute more than one-third of all caesareans in a given year. More than 90 percent of deliveries in which the mother has had a previous caesarean are done by caesarean. Yet several studies have shown that vaginal births after a caesarean are possible in more than 80 percent of cases.

Second are national comparisons. The U.S. caesarean rate is twice the rate of the Netherlands and more than twice the rate of Norway. These are countries whose infant mortality rates are similar—if not superior—to ours: Could our real physical ability to birth naturally be so different from theirs? The caesarean rate in this country has more than quadrupled in the last twenty-five years; could our own reproductive apparatus have changed that drastically within the span of only a single generation?

A number of hospitals have reported that as they curb their caesarean rates, their maternal and infant

Figure 1

Caesarean Rates and Primary Caesarean Rates, 1982–87

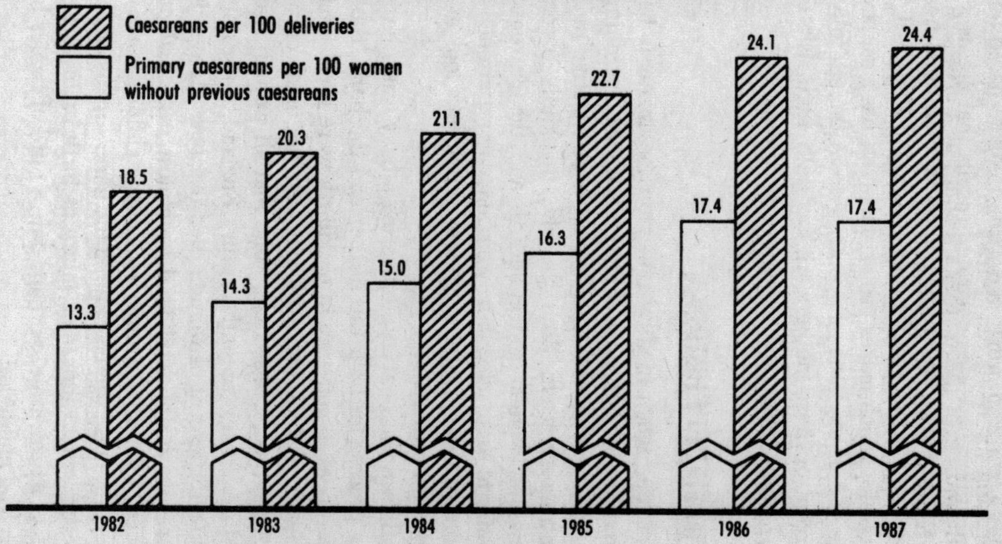

Caesareans per 100 deliveries

Primary caesareans per 100 women without previous caesareans

Year	Caesareans per 100 deliveries	Primary caesareans per 100 women
1982	18.5	13.3
1983	20.3	14.3
1984	21.1	15.0
1985	22.7	16.3
1986	24.1	17.4
1987	24.4	17.4

SOURCE: National Center for Health Statistics, National Hospital Discharge Survey

—5—

safety records improve. Similarly, midwife-based birthing centers have demonstrated results that are as good as and possibly better than those of traditional hospitals. The North Central Bronx Hospital in New York, for example, which makes use of midwives, has a caesarean rate of half the national average rate. Although fully 70 percent of these mothers are medically high risk, only 10.7 of the babies delivered go into intensive care.

CHILDBIRTH IN HISTORY

At a time when medical policy on caesareans is being taken to task and some of the excesses are beginning to be corrected, it is helpful to get a perspective on the controversy itself. Both the old, thankfully outdated views on women and childbirth and the current response to them affect how women today experience and perceive their childbirth options. First, let's look at the historical picture.

Before this century, delivering a baby was a hazardous process for both the birther and the born. Biblical references to suffering in childbirth were greatly taken to heart, and the inevitable pain and risk involved were regarded as "Eve's curse," one that all women had to endure. In seventeenth-century England, for example, some 15 percent of women died in labor. Many others were physically debilitated by almost perpetual pregnancy. Typically, women bore many children—six to a dozen or more was considered the norm—many of whom succumbed to illness or injury at birth or in early infancy. At this time, perhaps only a third of babies born survived childhood.

Obstetrics—the term stems from the Latin word meaning "to stand"—developed as a specialty in the seventeenth century, although doctors' attendance at births did not become widespread for at least another hundred years. But before obstetrics emerged, women generally delivered at home, usually with the assistance of midwives or other female helpers. When medical "advances" began to be applied to women's bodies, the results were often catastrophic. While a midwife would stay with a laboring woman, using her experience with births to ease the new mother through the process, a doctor would move from patient to patient, spreading infection even as he employed his medical skills.

There followed a virtual epidemic of puerperal fever, as women in European cities increasingly went to crowded, unclean hospitals to give birth. In one year, not a single woman in the province of Lombardy survived childbirth. Barely more than a century ago, 20 percent of the patients in one Boston hospital died of the fever. Some women would flee rather than allow themselves to be brought to the ward for their lying-in.

At the height of the Victorian era, there was great interest in the birthing habits of peasant and native women, who seemed to go through the process with little distress. (According to Paula Weideger's *History's Mistress*, some Slavic peasant women, seized by labor pains while working in the hills, would deliver their babies themselves, and then carry the newborn—along with a full load of firewood—all the way home.)

It appears that in the Victorian era, pregnant women of "higher culture" faced a tougher time than others in some respects, for a number of reasons. It was generally thought that any activity on a woman's part detracted from her reproductive "energies." Therefore, affluent pregnant women were discouraged from reading, working, and socializing. Pregnant women who could afford it were sedentary, and during the last several months of their pregnancies (a period known as "confinement"), many barely moved at all. Because of this, they tended to have large babies. Moreover, many well-to-do women were malnourished, tightly corseted throughout pregnancy, and ignorant—if not actually afraid—of their own bodies. By contrast, "mill girls" and other working women who were physically active throughout their pregnancies tended to have smaller babies and, consequently, easier deliveries. But many of these babies were *too* small and were born with problems. All in all, it was a time not conducive to childbirth for women of any class.

Typical of the attitudes of the day, the medical community threw obstetrical expertise at the deliveries rather than address these social issues. They did so blindly—literally, since doctors performed vaginal examinations and deliveries strictly by feel. (It was considered improper for a male physician to so much as look at a woman's body.)

In the United States, as gynecology and obstetrics emerged as medical specialties, physicians legitimized themselves by discrediting midwives and bolstering their own unique contributions to childbirth—namely, surgical tools. In the late nineteenth century, doctors came to favor the use of knives and forceps—a bias that was perpetuated in medical schools. Between 1915 and 1928, the United States' maternal mortality rate was higher than that of most European countries and more than double Japan's, according to Sarah Stage's *Female Complaints*. These rates were as high among middle-class city-dwellers, who had access to medical care, as among the rural poor.

Paralleling the trend toward medical intervention in

births were changes in attitudes. As doctors took over deliveries, women were reduced to passive participants in the birth process. As Adrienne Rich points out in *Of Woman Born*, the prevailing view among women was "Let the experts take care of it, I don't want to know what's happening." When childbirth became a medical event, women became patients, essentially waiting to be "cured" of their pregnancies.

It became a popular view that women were too weak to tolerate the rigors of childbirth. Up through the middle of this century, women were given what was called "twilight sleep," a combination of pain medication and a drug to make the woman forget what had happened to her. The message to women was that childbirth was a frightening endeavor from which they had best be protected.

Instead of enhancing and facilitating births, the emphasis came to be placed on *controlling* births. Women would lie on their backs, discouraged from moving about and making noises. It has been suggested that this partly reflected the predominantly male medical profession's discomfort with seeing women as anything other than ladylike. While in labor, a woman may seem to be overtaken by fierce—and, in the old view, "animallike" —urges (as happens with any strenuous activity—who could run a 440 dash without at least a bit of huffing and puffing?). The doctor's role, then, was to save her from this and provide her with a ladylike birth, which apparently meant being sedated and lying still with her feet in stirrups—just the kind of situation that leads to, or eventually demands, intervention.

All this played into the American love of technology in the middle twentieth century. Science could do anything, so why shouldn't it be used to make childbirth an easier, more controllable event? In an age of labor-saving devices, medicine applied itself to the childbearing labor of women. Artificially inducing labor became commonplace, so that women and their doctors could predict exactly when labor would begin and plan accordingly.

Certainly, recent medical advances have brought great reductions in infant and maternal mortality—not to mention a decrease in women's suffering. Yet it can also be argued that medical intervention has been carried too far, that the overall goal of better and more predictable results has subjected countless women, many of whom might be perfectly capable of vaginal labor, to surgery. As Doris Haire, president of the American Foundation for Maternal and Child Health, puts it, "A normal biological process has been made pathological by well-intended obstetrical practices."

CAESAREANS IN HISTORY

The history of the caesarean operation is tied in with the history of childbirth as a whole. Caesarean lore goes back long before the advent of modern medicine. There are numerous references to abdominal births in classical mythology and traditional legend. Many historical figures were said to have been born by abdominal section, including Scipio Africanus, the Roman general who defeated Hannibal, and Pope Gregory XIV. In Shakespeare's *Macbeth*, the hero learns that his opponent, MacDuff, was from his mother's womb "untimely ripped." This "untimely ripping" was probably done post mortem, for caesareans were generally performed to save the infant from a mother who had died in childbirth.

A law in late Roman times, called the *Lex Caesare*, mandated caesareans in situations when the mother's life could not be saved. This is probably the origin of the term *caesarean*. (It's not likely that Julius Caesar was delivered by caesarean section, since Caesar's mother lived to raise him; it is doubtful that many—if any— women survived the operation at that time.) Another possible origin for the term is the Latin *cadere*, which means "to cut."

The first caesarean in which both mother and child lived is thought to have occurred in Switzerland in the year 1500, when a sow-gelder named Jacob Nufer performed the operation on his wife. She allegedly went on to give birth to six more children (vaginally, it can be assumed; so much for the dictum "Once a cesarean, always a cesarean"). The first reported caesarean in the United States took place in 1794 in a log cabin in Virginia, when a Dr. Bennett successfully operated on his wife, the former Elisabeth Hog.

One of the main reasons the operation was so dangerous at that time is that after the birth, the uterus was not sewn up but was left alone to heal. So even if the mother didn't die immediately from uncontrolled blood loss, she likely succumbed to serious infection. Between 1700 and 1789, not one woman in Paris survived a caesarean delivery. In the nineteenth century, it was said, a woman had a far greater chance of surviving goring by a bull or surgery performed on herself than surviving a caesarean done by a surgeon. The best candidates for the operation were reported to be women who were, not surprisingly, "strong and courageous."

The safety record for caesarean births improved drastically during the twentieth century. From 1886 to 1986, maternal mortality from caesarean births declined from almost 100 percent to less than one in one thousand. A number of developments contributed to the enhanced safety, including the adoption of uterine sutures to arrest hemorrhage, the use of aseptic (contamination-free) techniques, and the shift from vertical (up and down) to lower-segment transverse (crosswise) incisions.

SOARING CAESAREAN RATES

While the availability of safe caesareans today should be applauded, their increased availability and safety may have led to the operation being overdone. For deliveries when forceps would previously have been used, a doctor today quickly turns to a caesarean. Caesareans, instead of being seen as a last resort, have come to be regarded as a way to "guarantee" a delivery when the outcome is in question. Unfortunately, there's no way to truly guarantee a birth, and as we will see, opting for a caesarean really means substituting of one risk (surgical) for another (vaginal birth).

A variety of factors have combined to drive up the caesarean rate, besides the quest for a risk-free delivery. One is that women today are having fewer babies and are starting their families later in life (when the incidence of diabetes and hypertension is higher). The pressure is on them—this may be their only opportunity for motherhood, so they want to make certain nothing goes wrong. A doctor may not want to take any chances in such a case, so he or she may schedule a caesarean. Probably reflecting this trend, between 1976 and 1986, the caesarean rate among women having their first child nearly doubled.

Another factor is the threat of malpractice suits, which have also become more numerous. A doctor may practice "defensive medicine" and choose to do the surgery to protect himself or herself, not necessarily because surgery is *medically* the best course of action. Doctors are typically sued for *failing* to do something, not for doing "everything they could." So even if a situation doesn't absolutely warrant a caesarean, a physician may feel that deciding *not* to operate may come back to haunt in the form of a lawsuit. The decision may be to do the caesarean to avoid this possibility.

Some people claim that the threat of malpractice suits is the leading cause for the high caesarean rate. However, Canada does not have a legal system that encourages lawsuits, yet its caesarean rate approaches that of the United States, so it's unlikely that malpractice alone can be blamed. Moreover, in the United States, the trend began before malpractice was much of an issue. But physicians are clearly on their guard in this respect. Obstetricians have among the highest fees for malpractice insurance—high enough that physicians are leaving that field and we may soon be facing a shortage of obstetricians. This is in fact already happening in some rural areas.

Changes in obstetrical training may also contribute to the increasing number of caesarean births. Obstetrical medical residents get little or no experience with vaginal breech deliveries, with external version (a technique used to turn a breech baby before term), or with the use of forceps. They do, however, emerge from their training very familiar with technical equipment and procedures.

Some critics of medicine point to greed among doctors as a factor in the caesarean rate. Doctors, they argue, opt for the more lucrative procedure of caesarean over vaginal birth. Some doctors do charge more for caesareans, and their reimbursement from insurance companies may be greater as well. The critics cite research showing that caesareans are most frequent when the payment is covered by private insurance and less frequent when the mother has no insurance or relies on government assistance. (Here the question can be raised of whether women with fixed-cost care, such as with HMOs, are getting caesareans when they need them.)

Other critics claim that doctors schedule caesareans because it is more convenient for them. In fact, it's unlikely that the timing of a doctor's golf game will determine whether a woman has a caesarean (as critics have suggested). But perhaps on an unconscious level, a doctor may perceive that a caesarean is "needed" when labor has gone on quite long and the doctor is becoming fatigued. Because the system today encourages rather than discourages caesareans, doctors are not urged to question their own motivations.

Another contributor to the steady rise in caesarean rates is the increased use of technical interventions. Electronic fetal monitoring, for example, measures the fetal heartbeat. As more is learned about interpreting fetal monitoring patterns, only those that suggest true distress should lead to concern, and even then the diagnosis in many cases can be confirmed with other tests. Similarly, dystocia (abnormal labor, or "failure to progress") is a common indication for a caesarean. Yet induction of labor, medications, or epidural anesthetics given during labor can disrupt a woman's labor and thus actually contribute to the problem.

This situation calls on the medical profession to question certain of its practices. First, routine repeat caesareans should be reconsidered. The recent guidelines of the American College of Obstetricians and Gynecolo-

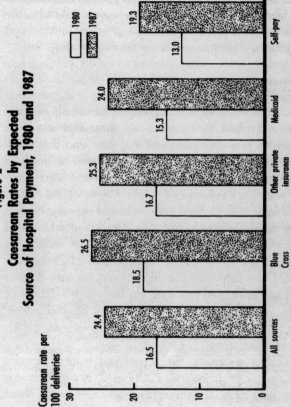

Figure 2
Caesarean Rates by Expected
Source of Hospital Payment, 1980 and 1987

Caesarean rate per
100 deliveries

- 1980
- 1987

	All sources	Blue Cross	Other private insurance	Medicaid	Self-pay
1980	16.5	18.5	16.7	15.3	13.0
1987	24.4	26.5	25.3	24.0	19.3

SOURCE: NCHS, National Hospital Discharge Survey, 1980 and 1987

gists on vaginal births after caesareans should have some effect on this. Second, it should be determined what constitutes *normal* labor, if abnormal labor is a common indicator for a caesarean. The natural variations in the pace of labor and the need for an optimal environment for labor have to be taken into account. Finally, the risks and benefits of medications given and procedures performed during labor should be evaluated.

BECOMING INFORMED

At a time when such disagreement surrounds caesareans—and when the chances are great that a woman may have one—it's more essential than ever that every expectant mother make an effort to learn as much as she can about the operation. A woman who is considering planning a caesarean should understand that caesareans have real physical and emotional repercussions; a woman who's already had one should understand that the aftereffects she's experiencing are not simply her imagination. Often simply being prepared for what may unfold can help ease the adjustment, because depression and associated problems are frequently related to a sense of not having control over one's life and health. Moreover, feeling that you're not alone can greatly lessen the trauma.

There's no reason for a pregnant woman to be a "victim" of medicine today. The medical community is becoming more receptive to women's concerns about the caesarean rate, and if your doctor is not sensitive to your doubts or questions and thinks you're out of line in voicing them, consider getting a second opinion. You need—and deserve—medical care that addresses your desire for a safe, fulfilling, and (if possible) nonsurgical delivery.

Despite its controversial history, the caesarean cannot be regarded as a weapon against women. It is an important surgical *tool* that, when properly indicated and properly performed, can be tremendously beneficial to a mother and her child. Even though it's often the traumatic, troublesome, and needless operations that we most frequently hear about, as well we should, there are a great many women and babies who benefit from it.

The case of Cheryl, cited earlier in this chapter, may in fact be typical. Rather than destroying her dream, she realized that her caesarean allowed her dream to be fulfilled; without it, her newborn son could have suffered complications. Throughout her pregnancy, she had taken classes and read books about labor, but she had also accepted the possibility that she might need a caesarean, even though her stated preference was for a vaginal delivery.

If, like Cheryl, you understand the operation and what it means, if you have a clear sense of your own situation and your needs (whether the caesarean is planned or decided upon suddenly), and if you have a doctor you feel comfortable working with, there's no reason for your own involvement with caesareans not to be a positive one.

CHAPTER 2

What's Involved in a Caesarean Birth

A caesarean birth is a delivery of a baby in which the mother's abdominal and uterine walls are surgically cut through, or "sectioned." It is also called a *caesarean section* or a *c-section*. It is a surgical procedure, requiring anesthesia and a period of hospitalization. After the operation, the uterus heals fully. There is no change in uterine functions, including menstruation, sexuality, or the ability to conceive. In the vast majority of cases, having one caesarean does not mean that the mother must deliver by caesarean in subsequent births.

There is one standard caesarean procedure, but a number of choices can be made within that basic procedure. Clearly, women who plan their caesarean births have better opportunities to discuss these choices with their physicians. But we feel it is essential that all expectant mothers understand the operation's variations. Because the need to do a caesarean can arise without warning, every pregnant woman should discuss with her physician what will be done if the operation proves necessary. By establishing your preferences beforehand, you can, for example, request a form of anesthesia that allows you to stay awake during the surgery and to hold the baby moments after his or her arrival. You also can decide if you'd like your husband to be present for the birth.

PREOPERATION PREPARATIONS

Knowing what a caesarean entails can make the difference between having a smooth experience in which you focus on the event of chief importance—your baby's entrance into the world—and undergoing a frightening ordeal that leaves you feeling that something you had looked forward to with great joy was seized completely from your control.

Many women who anticipate a vaginal birth fail even to consider the possibility of having a caesarean. In childbirth classes, they may concentrate on the breathing and pushing—the tools of labor—and virtually disregard any discussion of surgical deliveries, with the assumption that it won't apply to them.

Case History: Two years ago, Angela delivered a child vaginally. In preparation for her most recent pregnancy, she took childbirth classes—her husband had expressed an interest in becoming more involved this time. But any discussion of caesareans left her completely cold. "I've done it once already," she would say. "Why would I have a problem now?"

She went into labor, and her water broke. Upon examination at the hospital, it was found that her baby was a footling breech—feet first—a position that presents great risks during delivery.

When her doctor told her she would need a caesarean, Angela went into a panic. She had been confident —even smug—about her labor, and now came this surprise. If only she had given some thought to the possibility before!

When something seems alien or threatening, people tend to try to distance themselves from it. But since many normal pregnancies culminate in caesarean births, this is not the wisest approach to take. The moment when the doctor hails the anesthesiologist is too late for you to start thinking of how you'd like your surgery to proceed. In a true emergency caesarean, when there's not a second to spare, your plans may well be put aside. But even so, your wishes can still affect certain aspects of the setting and recovery.

Much of the apprehension people have before any operation stems from their fears of the unknown. But if you have a sense of what's going to happen to you during those blurry hours in the operating room, you can go into the procedure with clearer expectations and greater confidence. If you know ahead of time what kind of postoperative troubles you might encounter, you will be better able to deal with them. For example, if you anticipate having lots of energy to care for your baby as soon as you get home, you're going to be in for quite a shock—and quite a disappointment. If, on the other hand, you accept that you will probably be fatigued and a bit depressed, the ensuing exhaustion won't be as fierce a blow. Rather, you'll regard it as a temporary slowdown that you'll have to pass through. In addition, you'll be able to line up extra help beforehand, so that you won't be further burdened while getting used to your new baby and getting back your strength.

Aside from information, the best preoperation preparation you can give yourself is to make sure that when you go in, you're in the best overall health you can attain. The better physical condition you're in, the easier your recovery will be—and the lower the risk of complications. Maintain good nutrition during pregnancy, get ample rest and sufficient exercise, and (if you have not already done so, as you should have), quit smoking once and for all. This is not revolutionary advice, certainly, but it's important to follow nonetheless.

Every woman's caesarean experience is different, depending on where and under what circumstances she has it done, the state of her health, and how she feels about it. But most share certain common aspects.

HOSPITAL PROCEDURES

The optimal time for a planned caesarean is a few days before the due date, but this might be pushed up as the day approaches. Estimated due dates are often inaccurate, and the full length of gestation may vary from birth to birth. The operation should take place before actual labor begins—ideally, as late as possible, to ensure that the baby is mature enough to face the world. A sonogram may be done to determine the baby's maturity and size, and amniocentesis to check the development of the baby's lungs. If labor should start before a scheduled caesarean, you can use labor techniques, such as special ways of breathing, to manage the contractions as you head for the hospital.

The majority of planned caesareans are scheduled for the morning. You will probably be admitted to the hospital the morning of the operation—possibly the night before—and will have been instructed not to eat anything for the eight hours prior. This is to minimize the possibility of aspirating stomach contents under anesthesia, an especially dangerous possibility because a pregnant woman's stomach tends to empty at a slower rate. In an emergency caesarean, the mother may have eaten, so antacids are given as a precaution, since it's generally stomach acid produced by digestion rather than actual food that causes the problem.

At some point before the surgery, you will probably have to fill out a medical history. It's important that you furnish as much information as you can here, even though it might not seem relevant at the time and even though you're about to have an operation *and* a baby and the last thing you want to do is answer a lot of questions. People respond differently to certain medications, for example, so noting down any adverse reactions you've had in the past would be helpful to your doctor. Long-term health conditions that your doctor may not yet be aware of may also affect the course of treatment. You want to make it as unlikely as possible that a mistake or a misunderstanding could occur.

You will also be required to sign a consent form that grants your surgeon the authority to operate and your anesthesiologist the authority to administer medication to relieve you of pain. You may view this as a mere formality and be tempted to write in your name without giving it much thought, but this consent form should be taken seriously. It is your right to refuse treatment at any time if you wish, and you can state your priorities there on the off-chance that anything unexpected happens.

Remember, too, that while your doctor is obligated

to obtain your consent, you have a right to demand that this consent be *informed*—that you fully understand the need for and effects of any treatment you'll be given (see Appendixes B and C for the Pregnant Patient's Bill of Rights and list of responsibilities). This is especially relevant for childbirth, for no drug has been established as being unquestionably safe for mother and child during pregnancy. If you want or need time to think about it, you can ask to see the form ahead of time. But under no circumstances should you feel forced to give a doctor carte blanche over your body—or over your baby's.

As part of the hospital procedure, you will probably undergo a thorough physical with a number of tests to ensure your fitness for surgery. These will likely include blood tests, urine tests, and possibly an electrocardiogram. Your vital signs—blood pressure, temperature, pulse, and respiration—will be checked periodically both before and after surgery. Discuss with your physician whether you should donate your blood or have friends or relatives donate blood for you in case the need for a transfusion should arise during surgery.

"Prepping" includes having the top line of your pubic hair and abdominal hair shaved. This may seem an unnecessary unpleasantness (in the past the entire pubic area would have been shorn). But it is done to clear the site of the incision—the hair can intrude on its repair. Then the skin in the area is cleansed with iodine or an antiseptic. Because the bladder lies close to where the incision will be, a catheter is usually inserted to keep the bladder empty. Under an epidural or spinal anesthetic, the catheter will probably be put in as the anesthetic is taking effect. Under general anesthesia, however, it will be placed in the bladder beforehand.

ANESTHESIA

Depending on your delivery—and your stated preferences—one of three forms of anesthesia may be used. With *general anesthesia*, you remain completely asleep throughout the procedure. The chief advantage is that it's reliable and very quick, so it's usually the anesthetic of choice for emergency caesareans when speed is of the essence. So that the anesthesia can be used for the shortest duration, everything will be set to go the instant it is applied; the doctor will virtually have instruments poised over the mother's abdomen as she begins to breathe in the anesthetic gas. (Some people cannot have general anesthesia because of severe heart or lung disease or a specific allergy; if you have any of these conditions, you should discuss it with your doctor beforehand.)

Regional anesthetics, spinal and epidural, allow the mother to be fully conscious as her baby is born while sensation is numbed from the waist down. A local anesthetic is injected into the spinal canal. Spinals are relatively quick (although not as quick as general anesthetics) and are of short duration. This can be a drawback in complicated cases that require a long time. Though rare, headaches can sometimes occur after spinal anesthesia. Such headaches will usually subside after a few days, but they can be quite painful. To lessen the chances of this, the mother will be asked to lie completely still for several hours after a spinal anesthetic has been given.

An *epidural anesthetic* is given by inserting a thin plastic catheter into the epidural space which lies over the spinal canal. A local anesthetic is injected through this catheter during the surgery. Because additional anesthetic may be injected during surgery, the length of the operation is not a concern. Epidurals are sometimes given to mothers in labor, so the means of delivery can be switched from vaginal to a caesarean without changing the anesthesia. It can take up to fifteen or twenty minutes for an epidural to take effect, however. Another disadvantage of epidurals is that larger volumes of anesthetic are required, increasing the possibility of side effects.

A potential problem with regional (epidural or spinal) anesthetics is that they sometimes lower the mother's blood pressure. For this reason, the mother usually lies slightly to her left side—a position that tends to maintain blood pressure because it relieves the stress on the vena cava, the chief vein bringing blood back to the heart.

Local blocks are rarely used for caesareans because they do not provide quite enough anesthetic to free the mother from pain during the surgery. They have been used in emergency cases when it was necessary to deliver the baby before any anesthesia became available. Few doctors have much experience with them, so they are usually not even considered an option.

The anesthetic you get may be partly determined by which type your doctor is most adept with or by a particular hospital's policy. Some hospitals use strictly general anesthesia. At New York Hospital, for example, nonemergency caesareans are typically done under epidural rather than spinal anesthesia. You may want to check on this ahead of time and evaluate your wishes in the context of what's available. You may prefer a spinal, but if a caesarean becomes necessary in the middle of the night and the doctor on duty feels most skilled in epidurals, it probably wouldn't benefit you to insist upon a spinal.

Anesthesia today is generally very safe. All anesthetics do cross the placenta, however, and can therefore affect the baby. This is true even when the mother is completely awake. During an epidural, for instance, the drop in the mother's blood pressure that can occur may trigger mild fetal distress. Such affects seem to be limited to the short term. But because there are two patients receiving anesthesia—the mother and the child—it's important to determine which one is the best for each of their needs.

When given the option, most women prefer anesthesia that allows them to remain awake during the operation, thereby allowing them to experience their babies' birth. Some women, however, would rather be unconscious. If you are one of these, make your feelings known, and your wishes should be respected. Still, the more you know about and experience the operation, the more comfortable you'll be with it, both during and after. With epidural and spinal anesthesia, you may feel a slight pain or a mild sensation of tugging, but you can always be given more or a stronger anesthesia if it's needed. It's not possible, however, to do it the other way around—if you opt for a general anesthesia, there's no way you can change your mind once it's been administered.

WHO ATTENDS THE DELIVERY

The question of who attends the delivery is often determined in part by the hospital you choose. In most hospitals today, the father can be present at the birth. For many couples, this makes the birth experience far more intimate and satisfying—indeed, much closer to the vaginal delivery that they may have planned. The baby's entrance into the world is above all a family event, and there's no reason the mother should feel lonely or alone. Unless there is a true medical emergency, the father should be able to welcome his child if he and the mother so choose.

Expectant fathers, especially those who actively prepare to be involved in a vaginal labor, may feel excluded, helpless, and even frightened when their wives are whisked off for a caesarean. Those who become part of the process are likely to feel more positive about and less threatened by the surgical birth. Furthermore, studies have suggested that fathers who watch their children being born tend to form quicker and stronger bonds with them.

In the past, doctors bristled at the notion of fathers being present. Their concerns were: Why have an extra person in what might be an already crowded room? Who wants someone—particularly someone so emotionally involved—watching over their shoulder? What if the father should faint or feel ill? These concerns, however, seem not to be a problem today, and the benefits to the parents far outweigh any potential drawbacks. The possible risk of infection from the father was also often raised, but this, too, has proved not to be an issue as long as the father washes and wears the appropriate sterile garments.

It's important to remember that the father's role is not that of a curious spectator or a watchdog to check on the doctor's technique. Rather, he is there to be with the mother, to lend his support throughout the process, and to witness the exhilarating moment when the child is born. Physicians therefore often discourage fathers from observing when the mother is under general anesthesia, since she won't be awake to appreciate his being there.

Couples should be honest with themselves. Not every man relishes the thought of watching his wife being operated on. Some people are more squeamish than others, and the father may wish to be spared the visual details. Similarly, some women may prefer that the father wait outside. They may find the operation easier to handle if the medical aspect of the birth is reserved for the medical professionals. If either of you feels this way, accept it. If your husband or partner opts for the waiting room or if you want to be alone during surgery, it's not a statement about your relationship or your worthiness as a parent. It's best if you do what's most comfortable for both of you.

Many hospitals allow someone other than the father—perhaps a parent, a close friend, or a labor coach—to be present at the birth. For someone who wants to be there but doesn't want to watch, a drape or screen can be placed between the observer and the operation.

During your sojourn in the operating room, others will be in attendance. You will meet the anesthesiologist, who administers the anesthetic and monitors your heart and lungs, blood pressure, and fluid balance during surgery. Besides your own physician, there will be an assistant, often a resident in training if you are delivering in a teaching hospital. You will meet two nurses—one who assists the doctor by providing the surgical tools and another who circulates in the operating room and is available to provide instruments, suture materials, and gowns and gloves to the operating team.

After the delivery, a pediatrician may come in to look at your baby. In some hospitals this initial examination of the baby may be performed by the obstetrician or one of the nurses. Your physician and the assistant will attend to you by sewing up the incision and making sure everything is okay. Before the infant is handed to you, the baby will have any fluid suctioned from its mouth. (In a vaginal birth, this fluid in the baby's mouth would have been squeezed out during the passage through the birth canal.)

CAESAREAN INCISIONS

A caesarean operation generally lasts between 30 minutes and an hour. The actual birth is accomplished within the first ten minutes or so, or sooner if general anesthesia is used. The doctor must cut through several layers to reach the baby: the abdomen, the uterus, and finally the amniotic sac, where the baby is comfortably housed in fluid. With one hand, the doctor lifts the baby's head, and with the other, he or she presses on the uterus. As soon as the head emerges, it is suctioned free of amniotic fluid, mucus, and blood. The rest of the baby's body is delivered and the cord clamped and cut. The placenta, or afterbirth, is then removed. At this time, oxytocin, a drug that mimics the substance that promotes uterine contractions in labor, is given. This is to minimize bleeding and to aid in the contraction of the uterus.

The remaining time is devoted to sewing up the incision. The ovaries and fallopian tubes can be visualized. Then layer by layer, the surgical incisions are repaired, first the uterus and then the abdomen.

Depending on the situation and your doctor's judgment, any of several types of incision are used. There are two major surgical cuts—the one on the abdomen and the other on the uterus—and a different type of incision can be used for each. The kind of scar that will remain on your belly won't necessary reveal which incision was used to cut the uterus. If you have had a previous caesarean, the same outer incision will usually be used.

For the abdominal incision, the *transverse* or "bikini" cut—which runs along the top of the pubic hairline—is the most common. It is often chosen for cosmetic reasons (the scar that results from a straight-across cut is less visible). Some physicians feel that it makes for a stronger incision and offers greater comfort during recovery. It may also heal more quickly because less stress is put on it in movement.

The *vertical* or "midline" incision starts below the umbilicus (belly button) and ends in the pubic area. The main advantage of this abdominal incision is that it's quicker and simpler for the physician to do. In an emergency, a midline incision might be the clear choice. The vertical incision is also easier to enlarge and thus affords the doctor more room. This would be a factor if your physician suspects scar tissue from a previous abdominal operation. It may also be done if the doctor plans to perform a classical uterine incision or caesarean hysterectomy. (The latter is a rarely used procedure, in which the uterus is removed after the baby has been delivered. It is done only in cases of severe infection, cancer in the pelvic region, abnormal placental attachment to the uterus, or uncontrolled bleeding during the caesarean.)

For the uterine incision, in some 90 percent of cases the *low transverse* incision is used. Here the crosswise cut is completely contained in the lower segment of the uterus. There are several advantages to this type of cut. There's less blood loss, less risk of infection, and far less chance of rupture in subsequent deliveries. The uterine lower flap is not involved in contractions during labor, so there is less strain on the incision. Adhesions are less likely to form with the low transverse, and healing tends to be quicker.

The *classical* incision is a vertical cut in the upper part of the uterus. A *low classical* is an up-and-down incision in the lower part. Although the classical incision was the most frequently used cut in the past, it is less commonly done today because it presents the greatest chance of rupture in subsequent pregnancies. Uterine ruptures are still quite rare. (The incidence is about 5 percent after a classical incision, as opposed to one in fifteen hundred births overall and less than one in a thousand for a low transverse.) But a trial of labor is not done after a classical incision because of the increased risk. Anyone who has had such an incision and then becomes pregnant should definitely alert her doctor, for a caesarean should be done before labor begins. Any patient with a previous classical or low vertical incision should be alert for any signs of rupture, such as bleeding or lower abdominal pain, even before labor begins.

A classical or low classical incision may be necessary under certain conditions. One such condition is when the baby is in a *transverse lie*, a breech position in which the baby lies crosswise in the uterus rather than upright with either the back or the abdomen facing the birth canal. Other conditions are if the baby is quite premature (for example, twenty-eight to thirty-two weeks), when the mother's lower uterine segment may not be thinned out yet; if cervical cancer is present; or if another condition, such as uterine fibroids, serves to obscure the lower segment of the uterus.

Depending on the specific circumstances, variations

on these incisions may be used. For example, an *inverted T* or a *J* incision, in which a vertical cut is added, is used to make more room for a transverse cut if there is a difficulty in delivering a breech baby. Because of the vertical component of such an incision, it is treated like a classical incision with regard to subsequent pregnancies.

Women who wish to eliminate any possibility of future pregnancy may choose to be sterilized during a caesarean delivery, so that they won't have to return to the hospital for a second procedure. Sterilization is usually done by tubal ligation, which involves tying a suture around a loop of fallopian tube and cutting out a segment enclosed in the suture. It adds no more than a few minutes to the entire procedure. (See page 38 for discussion of sterilization.)

RECOVERY

After the operation, you will be brought to the recovery room. You will remain there until your vital signs are deemed stable and you fully regain sensation. If you have had general anesthesia, you may well feel groggy for several hours or even a day. If you have had a regional anesthetic, the feeling will slowly begin to reappear in the lower half of your body. People recover from anesthesia at varying rates. It must take its course, so don't berate yourself for "failing" your baby if you are too sleepy to appreciate him or her immediately.

Although you'll spend no more than a few hours in the recovery room, it may seem a lot longer, especially if you had anticipated spending this time getting to know your new baby. For many women, it is lonely there, a letdown after the high of the birth.

You will probably be encouraged to cough and take deep breaths soon after you emerge from the operation, because the lungs often fail to fully expand after anesthesia and surgery. The nurses on staff should be able to help you. Many women are reluctant to cough for fear that the incision will open up. This will not happen. Try holding a pillow or towel against your abdomen, which may be more comfortable for you. It's important that you work on your breathing soon after surgery, even if it hurts at first. The more you do it, the sooner your discomfort will fade.

After leaving the recovery room, you'll go back to your hospital room, where you'll spend the next four days or so. By the first day after surgery, you'll probably be able to take fluids orally. By the second day, you may be back on a regular—though light—diet, as long as bowel function has returned. (Under anesthesia—particularly a general anesthesia—bowel function tends to get sluggish and may require a few days to return.) It's quite common to get gas pains after surgery; for some caesarean mothers, in fact, this is among the operation's most uncomfortable aspects.

By the third day, you will probably be allowed to take a (no doubt very welcome) shower. On approximately the fifth day, the stitches or staples will be removed, if necessary. Some physicians use dissolving sutures, which don't require removal.

By the day after surgery, you'll be urged to walk. Walking helps to prevent clots from forming in your legs and to get your digestive system working again. You may find that at first your gait is not what it was and that you're doing a rendition of the "caesarean shuffle" (a walk with a decided lean). It's important that you take an active part in your recovery, even while you're still in the hospital. Try to move about and sit up. Do minor exercises like moving your fingers and toes, then work on your arms and legs. Regaining muscle tone and strength will help to increase the stamina you'll need to care for your baby.

After the anesthesia wears off, you will feel some degree of pain (although the pain is often much less pronounced after a repeat caesarean). In addition, all mothers feel afterpains from the birth, regardless of the means of delivery (because of the contraction of the uterus), pain from the incision, and possibly gas pains.

People vary in their perceptions of pain. Medication to alleviate it is available, but it's up to you to assess your needs. You don't want to become dependent on pain killers, but this is not the time to be a martyr either; short-term use of pain medication will not cause addiction. Keep in mind that you will be better able to tend to your baby if you're not absorbed by your own discomfort. If you're nursing, let your doctor know so that you'll be given pain medication that has minimal effect on the baby.

As to how much you can do for the baby during this time, be your own judge. Accept that you may not feel up to it for a while. This is perfectly normal—any operation takes a physical toll, and most of your body's energy is going into the recovery process. You can't simply *will* yourself into being a more active and energetic mother.

But as much as you don't want to exhaust yourself, you also don't want to feel deprived. Close and early contact promotes bonding between mother and child and provides a strong base for the new relationship. Ask for assistance so that you can be close to your baby without straining yourself. A nurse can pick the baby up for you; an electric bed can allow you to maneuver more easily.

Breast-feeding is a good way to establish contact with your baby, and caesarean mothers are just as able to breast-feed as those who give birth vaginally (although the milk generally comes about a day later). Allowing your baby to suckle soon after the operation can aid in your own recovery, as well as in bonding. Suckling triggers the lactation process, so you might be able to nurse your child sooner. And suckling releases oxytocin, the hormone that causes the uterus to contract. While you are recovering and still nursing your own pains, it may be difficult to find a comfortable position to breast-feed. Many women find that sitting up in a chair is the easiest.

GOING HOME

On the fourth or fifth day after the operation, you'll be allowed to leave the hospital. You may experience some symptoms after you arrive home. It's important to know what to anticipate so that you'll have a sense of what should and shouldn't alarm you and prompt a call to your physician.

For example, you can expect some incisional pain and a certain amount of discharge. This discharge will generally be bloody for about a week, then turn reddish brown. The reddish-brown discharge, which occurs for several weeks after delivery, is from the healing of the veins at the placental site. It often has an odor, and many women confuse this discharge with signs of infection.

Symptoms of infection or other problems include foul-smelling discharge, vomiting, fever, and worsening abdominal pain. These, and any kind of pus of discharge at the sit of the incision, should be checked by a doctor. It's normal for little scabs to appear at the incision, but pus or bloody drainage suggests a possible infection. Many women have numbness or puffiness around the incision, but this should go away by itself after a few months. But whenever you have any symptoms and questions about them, let your doctor know. The sooner any postoperative problems get taken care of, the better.

Case History: Two days after she came home after her caesarean, Bonnie developed a fever that hovered around 102 degrees Fahrenheit. She became worried that she had contracted an abdominal infection from the operation. She called her sister to take care of the baby, then went to the doctor. It turned out she had mastitis, a breast infection that occasionally occurs after any delivery and that is marked by breast pain, swelling and fever. She was given antibiotics to clear up the infection and was relieved to learn that she could continue breast-feeding.

Any change in family routine will tire you, especially a young infant, who wakes every few hours around the clock. But after a caesarean, you must adjust to this new life at the same time that you're recuperating from surgery. After about a month, a caesarean mother will catch up with the energy of a vaginal-birth mother, but those initial weeks can be trying. There are huge individual variations; there's no way to predict the pace of recovery. If you're dragging more than you think you should be, it needn't suggest that there's anything wrong, nor does it in any way imply that you will feel that way forever.

If your caesarean was planned, you can arrange for extra help ahead of time. If not, you can still draft someone to assist you—a friend, a relative, or someone hired through an agency. You don't necessarily need a trained baby nurse. You may prefer to take care of the baby yourself and have the someone else help with the cooking and cleaning. Or it might be possible for your husband to take time off. Some employers are becoming more open-minded about offering paternity leave, although the situation today is still far from ideal. However you make arrangements, simply knowing that you have taken care of things in advance will greatly ease the stress that you may confront when you face everyday life—plus one new baby—again.

Although the incision should hold, it's best to avoid heavy lifting and strenuous exercise for at least four weeks. Many doctors advise not to drive a car for about a month. (Some car insurance companies do not cover accidents in the first month after a caesarean or other abdominal surgery.) You should also wait several weeks before having sexual intercourse. (Other kinds of physical closeness and caressing are perfectly okay.) The main reason for abstinence from intercourse is the danger of infecting the healing uterus. This is true after either caesarean or vaginal birth.

When you resume sexual intercourse, you should practice contraception, unless you want to become pregnant again. Although you may have less of a chance of conceiving while you are breast-feeding, this alone is not a sufficient means of avoiding pregnancy. Even if you have not resumed menstruation, there is a chance that you can get pregnant. Use a condom until you settle on a regular form of contraception. This is something you should discuss with your physician and your husband. If you want to use a diaphragm, you will have to be refitted, as pregnancy alters the size of the vagina. There is medical controversy about whether the pill can be prescribed to breast-feeding mothers. If you're not nursing, you can restart the pill after your first menstrual period if that is your usual method of contraception.

Many women's health advocates are concerned about the increasing rate of postpartum sterilizations. Postpartum sterilizations are far more common following caesareans than after vaginal deliveries, particularly after repeat caesareans. It has been suggested that the operation may put some women off the idea of bearing more children. Other women might harbor the notion that it would somehow be dangerous to have any subsequent caesareans and decide to be sterilized on that basis alone.

The point about sterilization is that it must be regarded as a permanent change, even though it can sometimes be reversed with microsurgical techniques. It should never be undertaken unless a woman has given serious consideration to what it means for her. The fact that it's more convenient to have a sterilization done when your abdomen is already opened up during the caesarean than a few months later is *not* sufficient justification. This is something that you should discuss with your partner and your doctor long beforehand, preferably before you even become pregnant. Make sure that your immediate reactions to pregnancy and labor don't affect your decision.

HEALING

Recovery does not simply mean that your stitches take hold and the pain subsides. It's above all a period of healing that involves both body and mind. Your body has to adjust to nine months of physical changes as well as to the operation, and you have a new baby to get to know. Many caesarean mothers have emotional repercussions as well (see Chapter 7). For some, a period of depression or disappointment (emotions that are common after any birth) occurs during the hospital stay, often after concerns about the operation and the birth itself have passed and the woman is forced to confront her own feelings about it. For others, depression creeps in weeks or even months afterward.

In any event, you may need to work things out in your mind. This is particularly true if the caesarean was sudden and you had no chance to sort it all out beforehand. Try to understand why the caesarean was necessary. Assigning a physical cause can free you from blaming yourself—or from feeling angry at anyone else. Remember that some form of postpartum depression is felt by nine out of ten mothers, regardless of the means of delivery. It is probably the result of hormonal changes, plus fatigue and emotional stress.

The most important thing about your caesarean is that it brought a new baby into the world and into your life. True, you had a tenure as a hospital patient, but above all you're a new mother. Perhaps the means of delivery wasn't what you expected—Federal Express rather than Parcel Post—but you have a healthy baby and the promise of your own rapid return to health.

CHAPTER 3

The Five Most Common Indications for a Caesarean and Why They're Controversial

Case History: Janie had a caesarean because her baby was in a breech position. A month later, a friend told her that breech babies can be delivered vaginally. Suddenly, Janie became enraged. It seemed to her that, despite her doctor's assurances, she hadn't needed the operation after all. Why had this happened? Janie asked herself. Had she been weak to submit to surgery so easily? Had she not done the best thing for her child?

Fortunately, rather than hold in her anger at her obstetrician, Janie called her. Over the phone, the doctor explained that the current medical feeling was that breech babies are best delivered by caesarean, and she told her some of the risks involved. In certain situations she would have considered attempting a vaginal birth, she said, but since this was Janie's first child, they wouldn't have applied to her.

With all the controversy about unnecessary caesareans, there's a tendency to want to divide all the reasons given for them into "good" reasons and "not good enough" reasons. Unfortunately, the line can't always be drawn that clearly. (The one clear "not good enough" reason is a previous caesarean with a low transverse incision. An automatic repeat caesarean cannot be justified on that basis alone.) There are very few situations that unquestionably require a caesarean birth. Similarly, there are a great many situations in which a caesarean may well be the best mode of delivery, depending on the circumstances.

For example, a woman might be told that her caesarean was due to *cephalopelvic disproportion*, which means that the baby's head was too large to fit through her pelvis. Two years later, she may delivery a baby vaginally with no problem at all—but this baby is *bigger* than the first. Does this mean that the doctor wrongly performed the caesarean the first time around? Not necessarily. The baby might have been positioned in such a way that the mother's pelvis, given its size, could not have accommodated its passage. Whether the baby's head is flexed (tucked in toward its chest) can make a big difference in itself.

The point is that the legitimacy of a caesarean cannot be determined on the basis of the stated reason per se; the context of the particular situation must also be considered. The decision is generally a matter of balancing risks and probabilities. If circumstances arise that suggest that harm may be done to the infant in a vaginal birth, the doctor must be seen as justified in calling for a caesarean. It could be argued in retrospect that the chances were overwhelming that a vaginal birth would not have threatened the baby. But in today's medical and legal environment, a physician may be held liable for any infant injury that occurs, and the "better safe than sorry" approach prevails. It's not such a bad stance to take. If your doctor, to the best of his or her ability, makes the best possible decision regarding your and your baby's well-being, it's better to look ahead at the joys your healthy baby will provide than to look back and try to surmise what would have occurred had the doctor opted for a different course.

So rather than break down the good and bad reasons for caesareans, a better approach is to distinguish absolute indications from relative indications. An *absolute indication* is an undebatable one. A classical uterine incision in a previous caesarean operation is an absolute indication. A *relative indication* is one that calls for a caesarean in some situations yet allows for a vaginal delivery in others. Maternal diabetes is a relative indication—although diabetes, a serious disorder that affects a person's ability to metabolize carbohydrates, is an undebated diagnosis. (If the diabetes has been kept under control, diabetic mothers can sometimes safely give birth vaginally.)

What's important to keep in mind is that a relative indication is as "good" a reason to do a caesarean as an absolute indication, of which there are very few. Your chief concern is to have an absolutely healthy baby, and that's certainly not something you're going to look at relatively.

Here are the reasons most frequently given for caesarean deliveries, listed roughly in the order of frequency.

PREVIOUS CAESAREAN

The most common reason given for performing a caesarean today is the fact that the mother previously had one. In most instances, this reason has no medical merit. Unless the reason for the initial caesarean has repeated itself, there's no need for any subsequent births to be delivered surgically.

Elective repeat caesareans largely account for the soaring rate of caesarean deliveries, and these are the caesareans that can most safely be curtailed. Today, fully 35 percent of all caesareans are done because of a previous caesarean. This figure is up from 30 percent in 1980. As long as the trend toward doing automatic repeats continues, every time a woman undergoes a caesarean, all her subsequent children will also be delivered by caesarean. This could be one child, or two, or four—and the number of caesareans steadily climbs.

Research has found no health benefits in automatic repeat caesareans. Other countries with comparable medical-care systems consistently urge caesarean mothers to give birth vaginally in subsequent deliveries, and when they do, they suffer no adverse effects on their own or their infant's health. Although nearly 80 percent of pregnant women with previous caesareans should be able to give birth vaginally, at this point less than 10 percent do.

Automatic repeat caesareans came into play early in this century. At that time, the vertical or classical incision was always used. It was found that this incision had a tendency to rupture in a significant number (about 5 percent) of subsequent labors. Because of the life-threatening hemmorhaging or shock that could result, Dr. Edwin Craigin, a medical leader of the period, dictated "once a caesarean, always a caesarean" as the rule, and the rule was accepted.

Because the operation entailed considerable risk to the mother, it was not commonly performed and was used only as a last resort. Craigin wanted to limit the number even further by reminding physicians that every caesarean mother would be forced to submit to the risks in all her later deliveries as well. Today, well over 90 percent of all caesareans use the low transverse incision, which almost eliminates any risk of dangerous rupture. Yet Dr. Craigin's words have been used to mandate repeat caesareans for all women, regardless of the incision, ever since. Today, ironically, the risks presented by an unneeded operation far outweigh the risks of a vaginal birth after caesarean, including the risk of uterine rupture.

Fortunately, change seems to be in the works. In 1982, the American College of Obstetricians and Gynecologists issued a statement urging physicians to attempt vaginal births after previous caesareans. In 1988, specific guidelines for subsequent vaginal deliveries were set. Among the requirements is that a woman with a history of even several previous caesareans is not to be discouraged from planning a vaginal birth. Among the other requirements, a physician must be able to perform a caesarean, if needed, readily, and the facility should be able to have the resources and personnel necessary for a caesarean available within thirty minutes of any decision to operate.

These guidelines reflect a shift in the medical environment. An increasing number of physicians (though by no means all) are now willing to attend vaginal births after previous caesareans. Because their doctors are more likely to accept the idea, women who want to attempt vaginal deliveries after a caesarean are also less likely to feel like "guinea pigs." While the percentage of caesarean mothers having subsequent vaginal deliveries still hovers in the single digits, it's more than double the 1983 rate and more than quadruple what it was in 1972 (see Figures 3 and 4).

Case History: Pregnant with her third child, Leslie was a bit taken aback when her doctor suggested that she deliver vaginally. Her second child had been delivered by caesarean, she argued. Didn't that mean she needed another one? The doctor explained that the first caesarean was due to fetal distress, a situation that was not likely to repeat itself. Furthermore, in the worst-case scenario if problems did occur, she could always be taken in for another caesarean.

Leslie felt a bit apprehensive about the matter, but she accepted her doctor's contention that a vaginal delivery was ultimately safer for her and the baby. At that point, she and her husband became excited about the prospect of sharing in the birth. She had a fairly easy labor. When she learned from other new mothers that many physicians still balk at vaginal births after an earlier caesarean, she was thankful to her doctor.

Based on what we now know about the relative risks of elective repeat caesareans versus vaginal births, all automatic repeat caesareans should be seriously questioned and the circumstances thoroughly reviewed. It's important to remember that a previous classical incision (or low vertical incision, which is also sometimes done) definitely precludes a subsequent vaginal birth. Also, in some instances the medical records aren't available to

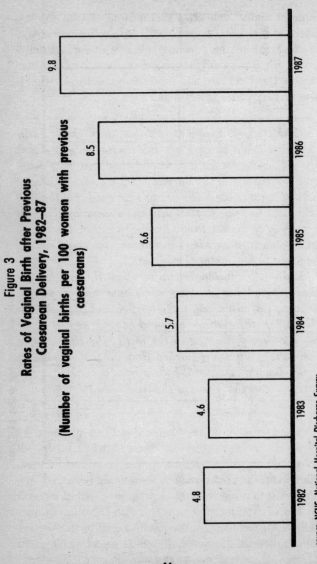

Figure 3
Rates of Vaginal Birth after Previous
Caesarean Delivery, 1982–87

(Number of vaginal births per 100 women with previous caesareans)

4.8 — 1982
4.6 — 1983
5.7 — 1984
6.6 — 1985
8.5 — 1986
9.8 — 1987

SOURCE: NCHS, National Hospital Discharge Survey

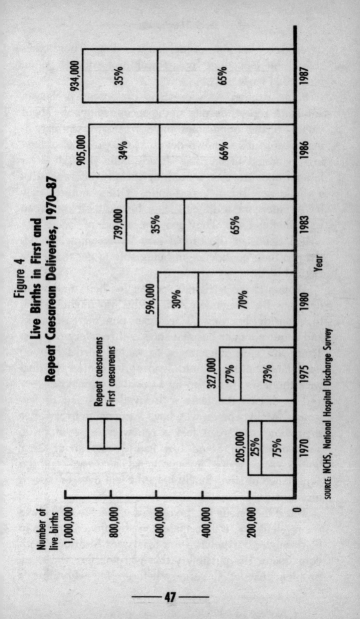

Figure 4
Live Births in First and
Repeat Caesarean Deliveries, 1970–87

Number of
live births

1,000,000 ─

800,000 ─

600,000 ─

400,000 ─

200,000 ─

0 ─

| | 205,000 | 327,000 | 596,000 | 739,000 | 905,000 | 934,000 |

Repeat caesareans
First caesareans

1970: 25% / 75%
1975: 27% / 73%
1980: 30% / 70%
1983: 35% / 65%
1986: 34% / 66%
1987: 35% / 65%

1970 1975 1980 1983 1986 1987

Year

SOURCE: NCHS, National Hospital Discharge Survey

determine what kind of incision was done. These cases should be looked at by medical professionals on an individual basis.

Some women with previous caesareans prefer an automatic repeat, despite all the encouraging news about vaginal births. Sometimes another caesarean is appealing because it's a known quantity; the prospect of having an operation one has already been through is far less intimidating than something entirely different, with a whole new set of uncertainties. Other mothers may have undergone a difficult labor before their caesarean was finally done. They may be afraid of facing the ordeal again, or the ordeal may have completely destroyed their confidence in being able to get through a vaginal birth.

Women have a right to a say in their method of delivery. But someone who feels this way might do well to reconsider her views. Caesareans pose increased risks and require longer hospital stays and recovery periods. There are clear advantages to vaginal births that no expectant mother should ignore. It's better to deal with the fears stirred up by a possible vaginal delivery and to discuss the fears with loved ones and professionals. Many women who have a vaginal delivery after a previous caesarean feel a renewed sense of pride and confidence. Some had had doubts about their bodies—often rooted in the original caesarean—and the experience of labor finally helped them overcome such insecurities.

But if the reason for the original caesarean is likely to recur—let's say, if a normal-size baby proved unable to fit through your pelvis—you may want to discuss with your doctor the possibility that you will face the same problem that led to surgery before. Not everything is predictable, but this might give you an idea of what to expect during labor so you can better decide if it's the best choice for you.

DYSTOCIA

Dystocia is something of a catchall word, meaning "failure to progress." Some 28 percent of all caesareans are done for dystocia, making it the second most common reason given for the operation.

This so-called abnormal labor refers to a number of different situations. The mother's contractions could be too feeble to propel the baby down into the birth canal. The baby may be too big to fit through the mother's pelvis. In some instances, the birth may not be progressing at the rate that physicians have determined to be the norm. The mother may be uncomfortable or distracted; simply altering her position or offering her encouragement could get her pushing vigorously again. Often it's a combination of several factors, such as a large baby and weak contractions. A large baby might have had no trouble squeezing through the mother's pelvis had her contractions been stronger.

Dystocia has become a rather controversial indication for caesareans. If "abnormal labor" is a problem, what is *normal* labor? Every labor is different, and long, short, difficult, and easy labors may all fall within the "normal" realm. Physicians often use Friedman's Curve to determine whether a labor has gone on "too long." Friedman, a professor at the Harvard Medical School, had intended his graph to show the great variations in the length of women's labors. Now, however, when a labor reaches the far slope of the graph, a physician may deem it "abnormal" and call for a caesarean for a failure to progress. In many cases, however, the abnormally progressing labor can be converted to normal by the administration of oxytocin. A pressure catheter may be inserted into the uterus to measure the exact strength of the contractions so that an appropriate amount of medication can be given. In this case, medical intervention may prevent a caesarean section.

Some cases of prolonged labor do truly warrant intervention. Once the amniotic membranes have ruptured —which usually heralds the beginning of labor—a delay in the onset of active labor means an increased chance of infection. This is because upon rupture, the bacteria normally found in the vagina can ascend into the uterus and affect the fetus. Doctors and hospitals may have their own policies as to how long they'll await a labor. Some regard twenty-four hours as the cutting-off point before some intervention, such as induction of labor, delivery, or administration of antibiotics.

The stage of labor in which the cervix dilates slowly is called the *latent phase*. This phase can last eight to twelve hours or for first-time mothers even longer. Studies show that many caesareans for failure to progress occur during this phase, although often the mother simply needs more time.

Medical intervention may play a part in this drama in a more negative way as well. (And many times, intervention is necessary—in a pregnancy complicated by hypertension or diabetes or a pregnancy two weeks overdue.) Once the amniotic membranes break, the meter starts running, and delivery is expected to occur within twenty-four to forty-eight hours. Sometimes, though, the doctor induces labor by artificially rupturing the membranes. (This can shorten actual labor by about an hour and give more predictability to the process.) If the membranes have been ruptured, there's no turning back. Oxytocin, a drug that stimulates contractions, may then be used to bring on contractions if they have not begun on their own.

Other factors can impede the progress of labor. Pain medications or sedatives, which can leave the mother sluggish, may also interfere with contractions or pushing. If labor does not progress satisfactorily, caesarean section may be necessary. Proper use of these medications must be determined on a case-by-case basis. The fact that a medication may contribute to the possibility of a caesarean in a given situation does not mean the decision to use it was necessarily wrong (see Chapter 5). Moreover, an environment that's tense and cold can get in the way of the mother's natural labor. This can distract her or make her anxious and actually interfere with the process of labor.

CEPHALOPELVIC DISPROPORTION

Cephalopelvic disproportion is a common cause of caesarean section, especially for first-time mothers. This is the condition in which the baby's head (in Greek, *cephalad*) is simply too big to fit safely through the mother's pelvis. Sometimes (though rarely) the mother's pelvis is exceptionally small. A woman who has suffered an injury to her pelvis—perhaps in an accident— might be in this situation. At other times, the baby is extremely large. Any baby whose weight exceeds 4,500 grams (about 10 pounds) has a high risk of not being able to fit through, and many physicians do automatic caesarean sections for babies whose estimated weights exceed this limit.

Usually dystocia derives from a combination of factors: when a particular pelvis cannot accommodate a baby of a particular size in a particular position. Sometimes the difficulty can be predicted early in the pregnancy. In the past, X rays were used to evaluate the relative size and shape of the baby's skull and the mother's pelvis. They are now rarely used because their accuracy in predicting who needs a caesarean is not very good and because of the potential dangers of radiation exposure to the fetus.

Usually, there's no way to tell for sure whether cephalopelvic disproportion truly exists until you go through the entire labor and allow the baby to deliver. If the baby does not descend through the birth canal, a caesarian section must be done. The baby's skull is still soft, and it naturally molds during the trip down the birth canal. Proper molding can allow for a large baby's passage. Similarly, during labor, the mother's pelvis is in a flexible state. The overall birth process is designed so that the baby and the mother's pelvis adapt to each other. A good labor with strong contractions can ease a delivery that would otherwise be problematic.

MALPRESENTATION OF THE FETUS

To be delivered trouble-free, a fetus should be in what's called the *vertex position*—that is, lying vertically within the amniotic sac, with feet on top and head on bottom, poised for the descent with the head flexed. If the baby assumes a different position, a vaginal delivery is potentially hazardous. This is because the head is the largest part of the newborn's body. If the head emerges first, as it does in the vertex position, the rest of the body follows with ease.

But if the legs or the buttocks come out first, as they do in a breech birth, there's no way to be certain that the head will fit. And any delay in delivering the head can lead to fetal brain damage, localized nerve trauma, or even death. Moreover, in a breech birth the chances of complications involving the umbilical cord are higher.

Breech births present increased risks regardless of the means of delivery. To keep these risks to a minimum, the vast majority of breech babies—about 85 percent—are delivered by caesarean. Fortunately, breeches account for only about 4 percent of all births, although they're slightly more prevalent among mothers having a first baby. Breech births account for about 10 percent of all caesareans today.

A breech baby can take one of several different positions. The most frequent one, occurring in about two-thirds of the cases, is the *frank breech*. In this position, the buttocks emerge first and the legs are extended, with the feet pointed toward the head. This breech has the best chance of being delivered vaginally in a woman who has had a previous child vaginally. In a *complete breech*, both the legs and the hips are flexed, so the feet present at the same time as the buttocks. In a *footling breech*, either one or both feet jut out first.

Sometimes an obstetrician can determine during an office examination that the fetus is in a breech position. In this case, you can discuss the situation with the doctor and determine a course of action. At other times, the breech position may not be detected until a vaginal examination is performed during labor.

Breech babies frequently turn themselves into a vertex position on their own. Many more babies are breeches at the beginning of their third trimester than they are at term. In fact, the more premature an infant is at birth, the greater the chances of a breech delivery.

In the past, premature breeches were usually delivered vaginally, since the baby was expected to fit through the pelvis. More recently, it has been discovered that the cervix may put pressure on the breech baby's abdomen, chest, or head. For these reasons, caesarean sections are now regularly done for premature breech babies.

Critics of caesareans argue that most breech babies can be delivered vaginally—and technically, they're right. If vaginal births, rather than caesareans, were routine for breech babies, probably more than 95 percent would suffer no ill effects. But that means that up to 5 percent may have complications, sometimes serious ones. It's this percentage that makes caesarean the delivery choice for many breech babies.

Vaginal birth may be attempted for some breech babies when the baby is in a frank breech position with the head flexed (tucked in toward the chin). Preferably, the mother has had a previous vaginal birth with a baby of about the same size or larger. A breech delivery should take place in a hospital, never at home. The physician assisting should be experienced in the delivery of breech infants, which may require the skillful use of forceps. Such a specialist may be difficult to find, especially among doctors trained in the last fifteen or so years, since vaginal breech births have been less frequently done.

Another possible way to handle a breech baby is to have the baby *turned*. The procedure, known as *external cephalic version*, has been used by a number of different cultures, including traditional American Indians. More recently in the United States, the procedure was used when caesareans were dangerous and every effort was made to avoid them.

In an external cephalic version, the doctor places his or her hands on the mother's abdomen and feels for the fetus's head and buttocks. The baby's body is then manipulated and turned until it assumes the vertex position. The entire process may take only a few moments.

Although this sounds simple enough, certain precautions must be taken. The procedure has to be done in a facility where an emergency caesarean can be performed if necessary. The mother is given medication to relax her uterus, and the baby must be watched by ultrasound and the heartbeat continually monitored. One potential problem is that the baby may be in a breech position because of a short umbilical cord. Turning such a baby could put stress on the cord, which could lead to fetal distress or other problems. And there's always the chance that the baby, once turned, will turn *back*.

The best time to do an external cephalic version is somewhere between the thirty-sixth and thirty-ninth weeks. This minimizes the chances that the baby will revert to a breech position.

Five years ago, external cephalic version were almost never done. But today, some professionals feel that there is a place for the procedure. If you choose to have an external cephalic version, go to a physician who has experience with the procedure. Since relatively few physicians are currently trained to perform it, you may have to get a referral to a medical center. You may also want to check on the physician's success rate, for doctors seem to vary greatly in their adeptness at external cephalic version.

Some experts contend that certain exercises can effectively get a breech infant to turn. One such exercise involves lying down on pillows so that your pelvis is higher than your head. In another, you lie down clutching your knees to your chest. Talk to your doctor or to a childbirth educator experienced in these techniques, if you're interested.

Another uncommon malpresentation is the transverse lie, where the fetus lies crosswise in the uterus. The baby cannot deliver in this position and caesarean section must be done.

FETAL DISTRESS

For most fetuses, labor is the most stressful time of their lives within the mother's womb. Up until then, all was relatively smooth, comfortable, and safe within the fetus's protective surroundings. With the onset of uterine contractions, however, the environment suddenly changes: the blood flow from the placenta may decrease with contractions; the umbilical cord may be pressed against parts of the infant's body or the uterine wall. Any of these can lead to abnormalities in the fetal heart rate.

The first sign of fetal distress may be an abnormal pattern in the fetal heart rate. In the past, fetal distress was detected by using a stethoscope to test the heart rate after contractions. This was generally sufficient to pick up the serious abnormalities, but some of the more subtle ones were missed. Today, the electronic fetal heart monitor keeps a continuous record of what's going on within the uterus.

The fetal monitor measures both the fetal heart rate and the timing of the mother's contractions. Two straps, placed about the mother's abdomen, pick up the needed information, by ultrasound (for the fetal heart rate) and by a pressure-sensitive device (for the contractions). The straps are connected to a machine that graphs the respective rates. Some variations in the fetal heart pattern are perfectly normal, although it may look alarming to the patient if the line makes an occasional dip or turn. Other patterns suggest that the baby may be truly stressed. If more information is needed, an electrode may be attached to the baby's scalp to measure the heartbeat accurately from beat to beat. A pressure catheter may be inserted into the uterus to measure the intensity of each contraction.

Fetal monitoring has been criticized for contributing to the increase in caesarean deliveries. In the early days of fetal monitoring, any blip on the screen may have triggered an emergency caesarean section. The result was not only unnecessary caesareans, but caesareans done under the worst possible conditions (hurried, frazzled, with everyone in an infectious state of fear). Today, however, professionals are much more skilled in the use of the fetal monitor. They know which patterns denote trouble and which patterns merely need watching.

When fetal monitoring was new, the presence of the monitor may have been stressful for some women. But this situation has changed, if nothing else simply because fetal monitors have been around awhile. Today, a mother who hasn't used a monitor in a previous birth at least knows of other mothers who have. Its mere presence no longer suggests cause for alarm.

In fact, many mothers find the fetal monitor reassuring. They can see for themselves that the baby's heart is beating regularly. A lot depends on the attitude you take. If you think of the monitor as a looming, mysterious intruder, that's exactly how you'll perceive it. But if you accept that it's there to ensure that your baby will not be among the small percentage of distressed fetuses, it's less likely to bother you.

Case History: When Rebecca went into the delivery room, her attitude was "No way! No one's going to hook me up to that machine." She imagined that she would be strapped down in an uncomfortable position on the machine, as if she were in solitary confinement in a futuristic film. Then she saw how the machine worked. She saw that she could take it off and walk around as she chose. So she decided to give it a try—"Just for a moment—no more." She found that she could hear the baby's heartbeat and see her own contractions even before she felt them. Knowing when the contractions were welling up proved helpful with her breathing. In no time, the monitor turned out to be soothing to her rather than an unwelcome intrusion.

The best use of the fetal monitor is not to send mothers to the operating room at the first sign of distress. Rather, it is to suggest which situations need watching and to follow a fetus's responses to different contraction patterns and interventions. The first step of a doctor who picks up signals of distress should be to take measures to alleviate the distress.

Sometimes merely changing the mother's position can correct a problem, such as when maternal low blood pressure threatens a fetus. Blood pressure tends to drop when a person lies on her back. So if she shifts to her left side (which reduces pressure on the major blood vessels) or gets up and moves around, the fetal heart rate may naturally go back to normal. In other cases, if oxytocin is being used, a decrease in the drug may return the heart rate pattern to normal.

The mother may be given oxygen, in the hope that by increasing the oxygen content of the mother's blood, the baby's will increase as well. Other methods of easing fetal distress are currently being evaluated, including infusing extra fluid into the uterus. The theory here is that if the distress is caused by the umbilical cord's being compressed against a part of the baby's body, the extra fluid could act as a cushion.

If necessary, a blood sample from the baby's scalp may be taken and the pH measured. This pH is a measure of acidity that gives an indirect account of how much oxygen the baby is receiving. The test must be done after the membranes have been ruptured or it will rupture them artificially. A normal pH indicates that the baby is not being severely stressed and is receiving adequate oxygen.

The test may be done several times to see if the chemical environment is changing as a result of distress. Fetal scalp blood sampling is painless to the mother and causes no harm to the fetus. Its chief benefit is that by providing additional information about the fetus, it can help avoid unnecessary caesareans.

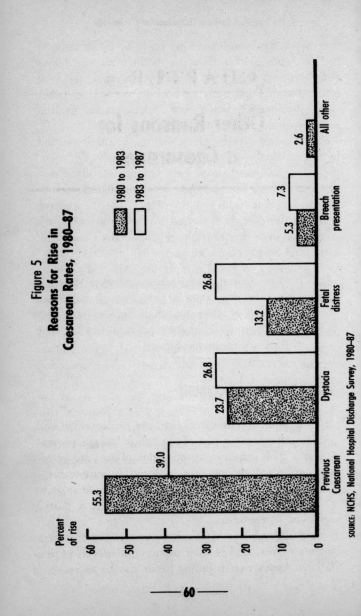

Figure 5
Reasons for Rise in
Caesarean Rates, 1980–87

■ 1980 to 1983
□ 1983 to 1987

Percent
of rise

Previous Caesarean: 55.3 / 39.0
Dystocia: 23.7 / 26.8
Fetal distress: 13.2 / 26.8
Breech presentation: 5.3 / 7.3
All other: 2.6

SOURCE: NCHS, National Hospital Discharge Survey, 1980–87

CHAPTER 4

Other Reasons for
a Caesarean

The "big five" reasons for caesareans discussed in Chapter 3 account for more than 80 percent of all caesareans. But any number of other conditions can also necessitate a surgical delivery. This chapter provides brief descriptions of the most common of these.

UMBILICAL CORD ACCIDENT

During labor, the umbilical cord can *prolapse* (fall out), along with whatever part of the baby's body is presenting first. This can cause compression of the cord against the cervix and severe fetal distress. In rare cases, a quick vaginal birth is possible, but in the vast majority of cases the baby will not survive unless it is quickly removed by caesarean.

A prolapsed cord most often occurs when the membranes rupture and is most common in breech presentations. Another contributing factor may be an excess of

Figure 6
Ten Leading Reasons for
Caesarean Delivery, 1987

	Caesarean rate per 100 deliveries	Rank
Disproportion	96.6	1
Abnormality of organs, including uterine scar from previous surgery	86.8	2
Malposition of fetus	75.7	3
Antepartum hemorrhage, abruptio placentae, and placenta previa	59.2	4
Obstructed labor	57.6	5
Infections, including venereal disease	53.2	6
Failed induction and other indications for care	50.3	7
Multiple gestation	49.7	8
Uterine inertia and other abnormal labor	46.3	9
Hypertension	43.6	10

SOURCE: Based on 1987 National Hospital Discharge Survey.

amniotic fluid, which serves to flush out the cord as the membranes are ruptured.

A normal umbilical cord is about two feet long. A cord that is exceptionally short may be pulled taut as the baby descends, and this, too, can threaten the fetal blood supply. A cord that's too long may wrap around the baby's neck or body. If the blood flow is reduced in the baby, fetal distress may result and caesarean section may be performed. In many normal deliveries, however, the umbilical cord is partly wrapped around the baby's neck without any adverse effect.

PREMATURE SEPARATION OF THE PLACENTA

The placenta provides constant nourishment for the developing fetus by serving as the exchange point for its and its mother's vascular systems. It usually remains attached to the uterine wall until the baby is safely delivered. In rare situations, it can partially separate either during the last months of pregnancy or during labor. This endangers the fetus by affecting blood supply, and it puts the mother at risk for severe hemorrhage.

Vaginal bleeding sometimes signals this condition. The uterus may become hard and tender to the touch, and there may be abdominal pain. Sometimes, the condition is signaled when a fetal monitor picks up telling changes in the fetal heart rate. The diagnosis can be confirmed by ultrasound.

The placental separation may be either partial or complete. Depending on the extent of both the separation and the amount of bleeding, an emergency caesarean may be necessary. If only a small separation exists and vaginal delivery is imminent, caesarean section may be avoided.

Risk factors associated with premature separation of the placenta include high blood pressure, smoking, poor nutrition during pregnancy, and advanced maternal age. In rare cases, placental separation could result from a fall or blow to the abdomen.

PLACENTA PREVIA

In placenta previa, the placenta does not lie at the top of the uterus, as it usually does, but becomes attached in the lower segment of the uterus. There the placenta blocks the cervical opening. When the cervix begins to dilate for delivery, the placental blood vessels are exposed, which can lead to more severe bleeding. The placenta also obstructs the baby's passage.

Placenta previa is usually suspected in middle to late pregnancy. Bleeding frequently occurs during the pregnancy; ultrasound may show a placenta lying low in the uterus in the second trimester. Sometimes a low-lying placenta will move upward as pregnancy progresses. Further ultrasound tests should be done in the third trimester to confirm the diagnosis. If placenta previa is still present, a caesarean may be scheduled before the onset of labor. But in other cases, as illustrated below, placenta previa can cause problems.

Case History: About twenty-five weeks into her pregnancy, Diane began to notice some bleeding. She went to her doctor, whose physical examination failed to find any abnormality. However, a sonogram revealed the problem: a placenta that was lying across the cervix. Diane was told to abstain from sexual relations, not to exercise, and should the bleeding start up again, to rest in bed. Ten weeks later, she started bleeding again and was admitted to the hospital. The doctor performed amniocentesis, which determined that the baby's lungs were mature. A healthy baby was then delivered by caesarean—a triumphant end to an unquestionably difficult pregnancy.

The combination of a partial placental blockage (called marginal placenta previa) and a rapidly dilating cervix may allow for a vaginal delivery, but when the placenta completely covers the cervical opening, a caesarean is necessary.

There may be a connection between previous caesareans and placenta previa. Multiple abortions or any other procedure that could produce scar tissue in the uterus can also play a role.

Whenever you have any bleeding during pregnancy, alert your physician. Not all bleeding suggests a serious problem. After intercourse, there may be bleeding from an irritation on the cervix; an umbilical polyp may bleed spontaneously; there may be spotting after a vaginal examination late in pregnancy; or a dilating cervix may cause a small amount of bleeding. But the possibility of a more serious problem should always be investigated.

BABY SIZE

Macrosomia (from the Greek *macro*, "large," and *soma*, "body") means having an unusually large baby. If the baby's weight is expected to exceed 4,500 grams (almost 10 pounds), a caesarean delivery is thought to be best. For one thing, an infant of this size may have trouble fitting through the birth canal. But even if the head can squeeze through, the shoulders may be of such dimensions that the baby may get stuck.

Two factors may contribute to exceedingly large babies. One is maternal diabetes. Babies of diabetic mothers tend to be quite large, often weighing upwards of ten pounds or more. Maternal diabetes may be either gestational diabetes, which occurs only during pregnancy, or diabetes that was present before pregnancy. In both forms of diabetes, the mother's blood sugar levels are too high. The fetus, whose own blood supply comes from the mother's, must produce extra insulin to metabolize the blood sugar. In this situation, insulin acts like a growth hormone. If the mother can maintain normal blood sugar through strict control of her diabetes during pregnancy, she is more likely to have a normal-size baby.

The other factor is that babies in general simply seem to be getting larger. This trend is undoubtedly tied to nutrition. Whereas in earlier generations, the amount of weight gain during pregnancy was restricted, today it's recommended that women gain twenty to thirty pounds, and many women gain more. Not all excess weight directly adds to the baby's bulk, but it does have an impact on the size. If a woman puts on fifty pounds during pregnancy, for example, this may increase her baby's weight from about nine pounds eight ounces to ten pounds. That can mean the difference between a baby that can be born vaginally and a baby that must be delivered by caesarean.

The best way to prevent this situation from arising is to be tested for gestational diabetes. If diabetes is detected—or if a woman has had the problem in a previous pregnancy—the growth of the baby should be monitored and the diabetes should be strictly controlled.

It's important to pay attention to nutrition during pregnancy and not to let the weight gain get out of control. You can ask your doctor or a childbirth expert for guidance.

A baby that's extremely small may have to be delivered by caesarean as well. First, very premature babies are more likely to have fetal distress or an otherwise traumatic delivery. Full-term babies that are smaller than normal—say, about four pounds at birth—also have an increased likelihood of fetal distress. Small babies may be caused by maternal high blood pressure and smoking, which in turn may cause other complications that necessitate a surgical delivery.

MULTIPLE PREGNANCY

The chances of needing a caesarean greatly increase with multiple pregnancies. For one thing, such pregnancies are often difficult for the mother, and the added stresses continue right up to delivery. Moreover, babies born in pairs (or trios, or more) are likely to be premature or quite small, and, as noted earlier, this leads to an increased incidence of caesarean sections.

Then there's the matter of position; the babies often lie cradled in the womb with one in the vertex position and the other in a breech position. Or one baby may be much bigger than the other, which may cause enough difficulties in labor that a caesarean is ordered. If the doctor suspects that problems could arise if one is delivered vaginally (such as a breech), he or she would probably advise doing a caesarean for both.

Triplets are still rare—they occur in less than one in eight thousand births. But multiple births in general are becoming more common because of certain fertility drugs now in use. When there are three or more infants waiting to be born, most doctors recommend caesarean delivery.

Regardless of the means of delivery, multiple births (especially three or more) require great skill and judgment on the doctor's part. Doing a caesarean alone does not take care of all the risks that such pregnancies pose. Thus, it's important that your doctor be experienced in multiple deliveries.

HIGH BLOOD PRESSURE DURING PREGNANCY

Two types of high blood pressure can affect the progress of a pregnancy: *chronic hypertension*, in which the mother has high blood pressure before becoming pregnant; and *preeclampsia* (toxemia of pregnancy), a condition marked by hypertension during pregnancy.

Both kinds of hypertension may threaten the fetus by constricting the flow of blood through the blood vessels. When the blood flow to the uterus is affected, the baby may not receive sufficient blood and oxygen, especially during labor, when other physical stresses come into play.

A slight elevation in blood pressure in the second half of pregnancy is not uncommon. Often, bed rest is the only treatment necessary. In preeclampsia, however, the elevated blood pressure is frequently accompanied by a whole set of symptoms, including fluid retention (which may result in rapid weight gain), protein in the urine, and perhaps headaches or visual disturbances. Severe cases may require some sedation and medication to moderate the blood pressure. Because severe cases jeopardize both the mother's and the baby's health, the pregnancy is often terminated by caesarean, even if the infant is premature. If the hypertensive mother has a cervix that is sufficiently dilated for normal labor, the baby may be delivered vaginally.

Eclampsia is an intensification of the symptoms of preeclampsia, with the additional symptom of convulsions. Because of the seriousness of the condition, the baby must be delivered immediately. Eclampsia often develops from preeclampsia but can also crop up seemingly without warning.

Among women who suffer from neither chronic hypertension nor kidney disease, preeclampsia and eclampsia usually do not recur after the pregnancy is over or in subsequent pregnancies.

DIABETES

Diabetes is a disease of the endocrine system that affects the metabolism, especially the metabolism of carbohydrates. There are two basic types of diabetes that may affect pregnancy. Juvenile or insulin-dependent diabetes usually begins during childhood and requires insulin injections. *Gestational diabetes* arises during pregnancy and disappears after delivery.

Women with juvenile diabetes mellitus depend on daily insulin injections to maintain their blood sugar levels. In order to decrease the incidence of birth defects, the diabetes must be strictly controlled from the time of conception. Pregnancy alters a diabetic woman's bodily functions and dietary needs, and it becomes even more essential that her blood sugar levels be carefully and consistently monitored, to make sure they are within normal limits. This demands a high level of effort and responsibility on both the woman's part and the doctor's. But this difficult situation is nonetheless a great improvement over the situation just a few decades ago, when most women with this type of diabetes were unable to have children at all.

Any diabetic woman considering pregnancy should be extremely cautious about her blood sugar levels and other complications before she becomes pregnant. Prior to conception she should consult with a physician experienced in following diabetic pregnancies.

During pregnancy, 2 to 6 percent of women develop a temporary form of diabetes that seems to disappear after delivery as suddenly as it arose. But gestational diabetes does present dangers, and all expectant mothers should be tested for the disorder somewhere between the twenty-fourth and twenty-sixth week of pregnancy. If a woman tests positive, she must be immediately put on a dietary regimen. If her blood sugar cannot be controlled by diet alone, insulin treatment may be necessary.

Risk factors for gestational diabetes include obesity, a family history of diabetes, previous gestational diabetes, a history of obstetrical complications (such as previous miscarriages, stillbirths, or large babies) or having been a large baby herself. A woman who is thought to be at high risk may be tested more than once during pregnancy.

If all these forms of diabetes don't receive the proper treatment, the risks of late fetal death, stillbirth, and excessively large babies can be significantly increased. Complications may occur toward the very end of pregnancy. The abnormal blood sugar levels may cause an imbalance in body salts (or electrolytes), which may in turn cause cardiac disturbances and fetal death. Therefore, if a woman with gestational diabetes reaches her due date and labor has not begun, either an induction of labor or a caesarean is recommended. For a woman with long-standing diabetes, a caesarean delivery would be planned in the month preceding the due date and after the baby's lungs are mature, depending on the severity of her condition and how well it has been controlled.

Another reason diabetic mothers are prone to have caesareans is that their babies tend to be quite large. As noted, this can be prevented by maintaining normal blood sugar levels throughout pregnancy.

With today's improved self-monitoring and testing, obstetricians are increasingly likely to allow a pregnant diabetic to go to full term and often to a vaginal delivery. From the midtrimester on, however, all fetal movements and changes in blood sugar levels are quite carefully watched. If any fetal stress is revealed and if tests show that the baby has reached maturity, the doctor will likely induce labor or perform a caesarean section to guard against any potential damage.

ADVANCED MATERNAL AGE

Advanced maternal age (thirty-five or older) is not in itself sufficient justification for a caesarean. In the past, it was assumed that these mothers, especially if giving birth for the first time, were at special risk and that caesareans should therefore be done as a precaution (see Figure 7). But if a woman has previously had a normal pregnancy and shows all signs of having a normal labor, there's no reason for her not to deliver her baby vaginally, regardless of age. Many physicians regard a healthy forty-year-old first-time mother who maintains good exercise and nutritional habits as a good labor prospect.

But the caesarean rate for older mothers does tend to be higher for definite reasons. Older mothers are more likely to suffer from medical problems that could complicate pregnancy, such as hypertension and diabetes. Moreover, the incidence of dystocia—the failure of labor to progress—increases with age. This may be the result of weakened muscle tone in the uterus, leading to less efficient contractions.

Just as frequently, however, it's a matter of attitude. A doctor may fear that this pregnancy is the woman's "last chance" to be a mother and think that a caesarean could minimize the possibility of anything going awry. Now that more women are starting families in their thirties and even in their early to midforties, it's becoming clear that older mothers can have healthy vaginal deliveries (unless of course there's a medical reason not to).

Case History: Janine was forty-one when she became pregnant with her first child. In her first prenatal visit, her physician said, "At your age, of course we'll deliver the baby by caesarean." Janine was stunned, and the words at your age *stuck in her mind. Her doctor's argument ("This way we know there won't be any problem") failed to convince her, and she consulted another physician, a woman who had delivered a friend's child the year before.*

"You're healthy and in excellent shape," the second doctor assured Janine. "There's no reason not to plan a vaginal birth, although down the road we may yet see cause for a caesarean." Janine felt satisfied with this doctor's approach and continued with her. A few months later, she delivered a boy in a short, uncomplicated labor.

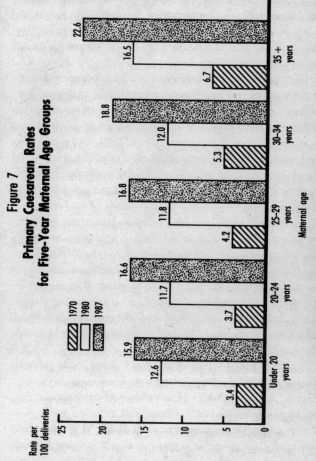

Figure 7
Primary Caesarean Rates
for Five-Year Maternal Age Groups

Rate per
100 deliveries

1970
1980
1987

Under 20 years	20-24 years	25-29 years	30-34 years	35 + years
3.4	3.7	4.2	5.3	6.7
12.6	11.7	11.8	12.0	16.5
15.9	16.6	16.8	18.8	22.6

Maternal age

SOURCE: NCHS, National Hospital Discharge Survey, 1970, 1980, and 1987

——73——

GENITAL HERPES

If an expectant mother has genital herpes, there's a chance she will need a caesarean. An active herpes infection, even one that is little more than an occasional nuisance or that is a source of only mild discomfort, could have dire effects on a newborn baby who comes into contact with the virus during delivery. If the herpes infection is active at the time of delivery, the baby could develop a serious, even life-threatening infection.

These complications are possible *only* if the infection is in its active phase. A woman with a history of herpes with no active infection poses no untoward hazards to the baby during the trip down the birth canal.

The chance of a mother's transmitting the infection to the baby is much higher during her initial outbreak of herpes than during a later flare-up of the recurrent infection. Initial outbreaks are exceptionally severe, so it's especially important that you not contract it during pregnancy, particularly as term approaches. Take extra precautions to avoid exposing yourself to the virus if your sexual partner has herpes and you do not.

If you or your husband have a history of herpes outbreaks, you should let your doctor know. Many doctors do routine weekly herpes cultures, but it's questionable whether they are necessary, since it takes a couple of days to get the results and the test can't be done during active labor. Therefore, the patient's clinical history and the doctor's visual examination are important.

You should minimize life-style factors that could lead to an outbreak during delivery, such as stress or extreme fatigue. If an outbreak does occur close to term, let your doctor know so a caesarean section may be planned if there is not time for the infection to be completely cleared up prior to delivery.

Herpes is very common, increasingly common, and no one should feel embarrassed to raise the issue with a doctor. Some women do not tell their physicians about previous herpes. Unfortunately, what they gain in pride, they lose in terms of added risk to their babies.

OVERDUE BABY

A pregnancy that goes on for more than two weeks beyond the expected due date, or about forty-two weeks in total, may be reason for concern. The placenta may begin to deteriorate, leaving the baby without its source of nourishment.

Frequently, "lateness" is simply a matter of an initial miscalculation in the due date. The first step is to verify the due date. If a woman has a twenty-eight-day menstrual cycle, conception would have occurred on about day fourteen. If her cycle runs thirty-six days, however, conception would have occurred around the twenty-second day of her cycle. Sonograms are often done early in the pregnancy to confirm the due date.

Sometimes the baby just needs more time. Given the normal variations in gestation length, about 10 percent of pregnancies extend past the forty-second week. In the vast majority of cases, everything is fine, just slow.

Beginning at about a week past the determined due date, the fetus can be tested for ill effects. In the past, the mother's blood and urine were assayed for pregnancy-related hormones; a drop in the levels was considered a warning sign. Today, instead, biophysical tests are performed on the fetus. A nonstress test may be done to watch for the acceleration of the fetal heartbeat after fetal movement, indicating fetal well-being. The contraction stress test may be done to see if the fetal heart rate decelerates after the mother's contraction, indicating the potential for stress during labor. Ultrasound studies can assess fetal breathing and the amount of amnionic fluid. Doppler studies monitor the blood from the placenta to the fetal blood vessels. All of these studies are designed to look for signs that the baby is outgrowing the fetal blood supply and is under stress. If any problems are apparent, labor can be induced. If induced labor fails, a caesarean may be warranted.

PREVIOUS PELVIC SURGERY AND PREVIOUS UTERINE DISORDER

If the mother has had previous surgery that required cutting deep into the interior uterine wall (perhaps to correct a congenital abnormality of the uterus or to remove deeply embedded fibroids), a caesarean may be necessary. This is because the scar in the uterus, like a scar resulting from a classical uterine incision for a caesarean, could rupture during vaginal labor.

For women who have had bladder or rectal repairs, a vaginal delivery could stress these organs, and so a caesarean may be indicated.

Uterine disorders that were not addressed before pregnancy may require that the baby be delivered by caesarean. For example, a uterine fibroid may cause a problem in a vaginal delivery by blocking the baby's exit into the birth canal. If a Pap smear and biopsy reveal invasive cancer of the cervix, a caesarean combined with a radical hysterectomy may be done to deliver the baby and treat the disease at the same time.

Not all gynecological surgery affects caesareans. Surgery for ovarian cysts, for example, has no bearing on a woman's ability to have a vaginal delivery.

CHAPTER 5

Avoiding a Caesarean: The Right Doctor and the Right Hospital

It should be emphasized at the outset that there is no way to avoid having a caesarean delivery if a baby cannot be safely delivered vaginally. You can plan to give birth at home with all the appropriate attendants (never my recommendation, however), but if the baby will not fit through the birth canal, you'll soon be on your way to the hospital for a caesarean.

But there are two things you can do to lower the odds of having a caesarean. You can slightly lessen your chances of *needing* a caesarean by taking the best care of your health during your pregnancy and by meeting regularly with your obstetrician. And you can lessen your chances of having an *unnecessary* caesarean by putting yourself in a position that favors a normal vaginal birth. Certain factors you can control.

Many books try to make the point that childbirth is either natural or medical—and that one is good and the other is bad. It has been argued—rightly—that one medical intervention can lead to another. A woman may increase her chances of a caesarean section by arriving at the hospital too early in labor and demanding pain medication. By putting her in bed and giving her medication, the labor may progress more slowly than normal. The slow labor may prompt the physician to rupture the membranes artificially or administer oxytoxin. An epidural may be given for pain relief, and this may interfere with the progression of labor and the mother's urge to push. Finally, a caesarean section is done.

But this chain of events doesn't have to happen. Childbirth, natural or otherwise, is rarely an all-or-nothing issue. It is true that medical advances have to some extent detached childbirth and labor from the natural realm. As we learn more about the relative risks of certain procedures, medical knowledge can be applied more judiciously so that it works with nature rather than against it. If a labor employing invasive measures does culminate in a caesarean birth, it's difficult to determine whether the caesarean would have been required had they not been used. In the scenario described above, the only circumstance that would alter the course of events, however, is for the woman to stay home longer, waiting for more advanced labor. Or if she arrived early, she could have been allowed to walk, refused medication, or have been sent home.

In other words, specific medical treatments—even if not wholly "natural"—may actually *enhance* your chances of delivering vaginally if they are used to attend to an obstetrical problem before it becomes bigger and requires a caesarean. Ironically, aggressive management of labor using invasive techniques can actually *prevent* a caesarean.

This, of course, presupposes that physicians limit their interventions to this purpose. Once again, it is crucial to have a physician who appreciates the way you feel about labor. A physician who shares your goal of an uncomplicated vaginal birth can apply specific medical techniques to bring that goal about. There is so much you can't control—what position the baby will decide to assume; whether the cord prolapses; and so on. But knowing that your physician is with you will ensure that if invasive measures are taken, they're taken with your goals—and above all the best interests of you and your child—in mind.

If you want to minimize your chances of having a caesarean, here are some steps you can take.

FIND THE RIGHT DOCTOR

The importance of finding the right doctor for you cannot be emphasized enough. Studies show that a major determinant of whether a woman has a caesarean is the caesarean rate of the doctor. Two doctors at the same hospital with the same type of patients can differ markedly in how often they perform caesareans. Over time, a doctor's caesarean rate reveals the kinds of decisions he or she makes about caesareans. Is the doctor willing to wait to see how a particularly stubborn labor progresses? Does he or she support the idea of having a vaginal birth after a previous caesarean? If a woman in labor complains of being uncomfortable, does the doctor quickly recommend medication or an epidural, or does he or she offer the woman encouragement and help her pull through?

The doctor's record over a short period may not provide an accurate picture. A few problematic pregnancies in a given month could skew the average. The kind of practice the doctor has can also distort the picture: an obstetrician with a sizable proportion of high-risk births might have an inflated caesarean record that fails to reflect the way he or she actually practices medicine.

If a doctor has a low caesarean rate, it's doubtful that this means he or she isn't doing enough caesareans. But if you're choosing a doctor to avoid a caesarean, it's important to be realistic. No doctor can perform miracles, and all expectant mothers, no matter how healthy the pregnancy, are at some risk for a caesarean. A doctor's low caesarean rate is a probability based on a percentage, not a guarantee.

The Right Doctor

How do you find such a doctor? If you already have an obstetrician/gynecologist that you're happy with, chances are you need look no further. But keep in mind that you're going to be dealing with this person far more than you have been in the past. A pregnant woman typically sees her obstetrician every three or four weeks up to the seventh month, then every two to three weeks, and probably once a week for the last month or so. Any problems or concerns make it even more often. So you want someone you don't mind seeing ten to twenty times.

The physician who is adequate to do your annual gynecological exam may not be the person best suited to deliver your baby. You should consider your doctor as if you were meeting him or her for the first time, since your needs and concerns are now different from the ones you had before. Obstetrics and gynecology once went hand in hand, but with medicine's increased specialization, more and more doctors are limiting their practice to one or the other. Even if you have a favorite gynecologist, then, you may have to have a different obstetrician to tend to your pregnancy.

Once you've found one, you're not stuck with any given doctor, nor are you legally bound to a medical provider who's helped you in the past. If you're not pleased with your doctor's treatment or approach, feel free to look elsewhere. Esther Zorn, founder of the Cesarean Prevention Movement, decided to change doctors when she was eight and a half months pregnant, after it became clear to her that her doctor was not going to allow a vaginal birth because of an earlier caesarean. Though clearly inconvenient, it was a move Mrs. Zorn did not in the least bit regret. It would have been better, however, to make the decision earlier in pregnancy. There is a bonding process that occurs during pregnancy between doctor and patient, and the trust, goals, and input of each can be conveyed during the months of pregnancy.

If you're convinced that what you're looking for is reasonable (such as a vaginal delivery after a caesarean) yet the doctors you meet are less than encouraging, don't give up. Caesarean support groups and organizations (listed in Chapter 8) can help you find an accommodating physician in your area. If you live in an area where medical options are limited, you can still make arrangements, like staying with friends or relatives if they live in a city with a wider range of facilities.

In seeking out a new doctor, either upon moving into a community or to replace one that didn't suit you, you need above all to consider medical competence and expertise. Make sure that the doctor has been certified by the American Board of Obstetrics and Gynecology. This alone is no guarantee of excellence, but it suggests a level of proficiency and training. It's also helpful to check with local sources, such as the county medical society, a family doctor, or friends.

The fact that a friend thinks the world of a certain doctor does not mean that this is the doctor for you. Your chemistry with a professional may differ from someone else's. Some women feel more at ease with a female obstetrician; others prefer a male one. You may like a doctor with a more relaxed style; someone else may prefer one who appears more businesslike.

Interviewing Doctors

You should go into your first or any meeting with a doctor with an open mind. Like any interpersonal relationship, you have to put some effort into your relationship with your doctor—and it takes both people involved to make it work. Many experts suggest that you bring in a list of questions to use as a guide to "shop" for the best doctor. While it is important that you get some information and clarify certain issues, there are two drawbacks to this approach. First, you don't want to start out in an antagonistic manner, but sometimes the twenty-questions technique can create one. Second, even if you ask all the questions on your list, you may not get a full sense of the doctor's style and attitude. If you asked the same list of questions of ten different doctors and compared their answers, the one that appears to be the best doctor on paper may not turn out to be the best one in practice.

Another factor you need to consider is how a doctor

practices. Does he or she work alone, or in a group practice where a number of doctors rotate night shifts? Many women balk at developing a trusting relationship with one doctor, only to find a different doctor standing in at the time of delivery. But there are definite advantages to having a doctor in a group practice rather than a single doctor. A doctor who's called out for only one night shift in four is more likely to be well rested than one who may have just come from attending a birth at another hospital.

A lot depends on how the group practice works, too. Most groups try to make certain that all expectant mothers are at least acquainted with all the physicians in the group. In others, you would see the same doctor for all your prenatal visits, but after that, in labor, it's the luck of the draw. Your regular doctor then acts as your advocate. Be sure that your plans for labor are communicated to the group physicians. Also, find out if there tends to be uniformity of policy among the group members.

The advantage of having a doctor with an individual practice is that you're more likely to get the doctor you've been seeing up to that point for the delivery. But the chance of getting a covering doctor remains if your original one is unavailable or on vacation. If your doctor knows ahead of time that he or she may not be able to attend the birth, often a consultation with the covering doctor will be arranged.

If a physician you meet with is not forthcoming about the information you do request, that in itself should set off warning signals. You want a doctor who makes you comfortable and who is open to your views. Pregnancy is one case where a doctor does more than simply tend to your health. He or she becomes part of one of the most important and intimate moments you'll have, the one in which your baby is born (for dealing with your doctor, see Chapter 8).

PICK THE RIGHT HOSPITAL

Your doctor's attitude alone is no guarantee that your labor will be handled the way you'd like. The hospital where that doctor performs deliveries can have a great impact as well. Many women think that, aside from actual profiency of care, all hospitals are identical. But they are not; if anything, the differences among hospitals are probably getting wider as economic struggles force them to address consumer demands.

Just as the doctor who's most convenient for you may not be your best choice, neither may the closest hospital. First, you need a hospital that's fully equipped and that has the staff and technology to do emergency procedures on short notice. Most major hospitals do have this capacity, but smaller hospitals and those in areas with a low population may not. In such a situation, driving a bit farther to a more sophisticated facility is well worth the trouble. You can get information about a hospital's safety record by checking with your state or local health department.

Hospital Caesarean Rates

You'll want to know the hospital's caesarean rate. Hospitals vary tremendously in their caesarean rates, from below 10 percent to upward of 50 percent. A hospital's caesarean rate is public information, and you have a right to know what it is—especially since it can affect the birth experience you have. (See Figure 8.)

Do consider the possible reasons behind a high caesarean rate. It could reflect the fact that the hospital
draws on a population with a disproportionate number
of high-risk pregnancies. But it could also be the result
of certain policies that the hospital maintains, or the
attitudes that prevail among physicians there. By having both the safety record and the caesarean record,
you'll be in a better position to judge a particular hospital.

Privately owned hospitals tend to have the highest
caesarean rates, while government hospitals—including
military hospitals—generally have much lower rates.
Hospitals with one hundred or more beds are also
associated with higher caesarean rates than smaller hospitals. But these are complicated statistics to analyze. It's
often harder to do caesareans in small hospitals if physicians have to be called in. In fact, some small hospitals
may not be doing caesareans as often as they should.

Another valid question to ask is whether a hospital
has peer review. Peer review is essentially a system of
self-policing, in which doctors at a particular hospital
periodically meet and evaluate one another's work.
Merely being aware that their decisions are going to be
examined or questioned can make doctors think twice—or
think better—about doing a caesarean or any other
operation that is thought to be overdone.

You must decide both about the doctor and about
the hospital. If it's important to you to have a particular
doctor, you may not be able to have your choice of
hospital. But be open. Discuss with your doctor the
strengths of that particular hospital. For example, the
patient rooms may be unattractive, but the hospital's
neonatal intensive care unit may be unmatched. A

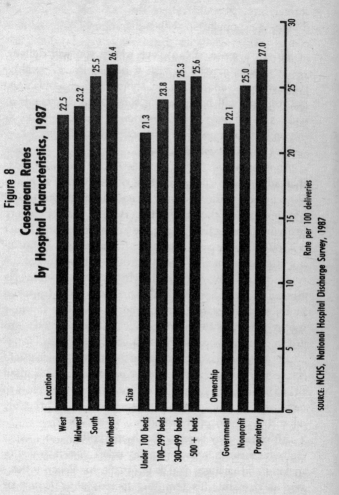

Figure 8
Caesarean Rates
by Hospital Characteristics, 1987

Location

West — 22.5
Midwest — 23.2
South — 25.5
Northeast — 26.4

Size

Under 100 beds — 21.3
100–299 beds — 23.8
300–499 beds — 25.3
500 + beds — 25.6

Ownership

Government — 22.1
Nonprofit — 25.0
Proprietary — 27.0

Rate per 100 deliveries

SOURCE: NCHS, National Hospital Discharge Survey, 1987

good physician undoubtedly has valid reasons for choosing a particular hospital.

Visit the Hospital

To get a sense of the place where you will deliver, ask questions as well as visit it personally. Preferably, both you and your husband should take a look. Since both of you will be spending time there, his needs as well as yours have to be considered. You'll be depending on him for a good bit of moral support during labor, so his comfort is no small issue.

Another reason that it's essential to see for yourself is that advertising and marketing often oversell a place. Whether they are for-profit or not, hospitals are run as businesses, and the maternity service is one area where many hospitals actively compete for market share. Don't rely on an impressive brochure. It may focus on appealing attributes, such as pretty gardens within view of the rooms, while downplaying drawbacks, such as an overly clinical environment within. Nor should you be taken in by such extras as private rooms or suites for new mothers or attractive settings. Pleasing accommodations are in no way synonymous with good medicine.

Be wary of a hospital's self-description, such as use of the term "family centered maternity care." This is often primarily marketing talk and doesn't have much basis in fact. Ask specific questions so that you know precisely what it is the hospital provides.

All of this may seem difficult and bothersome, especially because there are so many other decisions you're making and changes you're adjusting to. When a decision is stressful, it's tempting to look at a picture or hear a statement and say, "That seems fine. I'll go there." But if you're well acquainted with a place and confident that it meets your specifications, you'll be much more comfortable when delivery time rolls around, and it can also make a difference in the type of care you receive.

Hospital Regulations

Hospitals vary greatly in the rules that are applied to deliveries. Some spell their regulations out; others base them on tradition and prevailing views. Either way, you want to know how deliveries are handled and how rigid the protocols are. Which forms of anesthesia tend to be used, and under what circumstances? Are expectant mothers routinely given enemas (less common today than it once was)? Are intravenous fluids given routinely, and at what time in labor? Can they eat lightly or drink liquids during labor? Are they allowed to move around or not?

You'll also want to know who may attend the birth. Does the hospital generally ban the husband from the delivery room if a caesarean section is necessary? Does the hospital regard the siblings of the newborn child primarily as potential carriers of disease or as an integral part of the family who can at some point greet the baby? Many hospitals have visiting rooms or otherwise make it possible for the entire family to gather.

Another essential point is to find out how much contact you'll be able to have with your baby. Does the hospital allow rooming-in (letting the mother and the new baby stay in a room together)? Does it allow rooming-in for caesarean mothers? Does it make it easy for you to breast-feed as soon as you're able?

Don't underestimate the importance of the environment. Your mind and your body are inextricably connected, and surroundings that make you nervous or distracted could well affect your labor. What are the nurses like—are they rushed and harassed or caring and attentive? Will you have privacy? Is the environment pleasant, or is it harshly clinical? Does the hospital give the overall sense that birthing is a natural, normal event, or are new mothers made to feel like patients?

Midwifery

Some hospitals offer midwife services. While many people regard this as a "new" option, midwives are anything but new. Up until this century, when childbirth became the prerogative of medical doctors, births were invariably attended by midwives. The profession has a long tradition of encouraging labor by noninterventionist means, keeping the mother as comfortable as possible through the delivery.

Midwives normally have more time and fewer patients than physicians. They are also usually trained in noninterventionist methods. Some women who are uncomfortable around doctors may find midwives less intimidating.

Keep in mind that if the need for a caesarean arises, you will have to be transferred to the care of a physician. It's important that you find out how this is arranged. You might have to move to another room or floor or be treated by somebody whom you don't know. If you have an independent midwife—one who is not affiliated with a hospital—and you would physically have to get to the hospital in the event of an emergency, this could make the situation even more difficult.

It's essential that your midwife be certified in the field. Various organizations offer accreditation, but laws vary from state to state. You want to determine how your midwife was trained.

Support

You can arrange to have additional labor support, such as from the baby's father, a sister, a close friend, or a trained labor coach. It is important for somebody you're comfortable with to be there. Ideally, this is the father, but some men just can't cope with this. Everyone involved should be honest about what they're capable of, even if a man feels that in admitting his reluctance, he's letting his wife down. It's better to have someone who *can* offer support than a husband who can't handle the task.

Case History: Richard was devoted to his wife, Tina, and was thrilled about becoming a father. But the physical and medical aspects of childbirth left him quite squeamish. He tried to hide his discomfort from his wife, but their Lamaze teacher noted that he closed his eyes during particularly graphic films and suggested that the pair select another person as a backup. They agreed, although Richard felt awful about it.

Tina was very close with her older sister, herself the mother of three, and asked her to help out. The three practiced together up until the due date. Richard worked hard to psych himself up, but during labor he panicked and decided he'd better wait outside. Tina's sister came in, was a wonderful labor coach, and later assured Richard that his response was in no way a reflection of his worthiness as a father.

Alternative Sites

One alternative site for delivering a baby is a birthing center. A birthing center that is located in a hospital or is attached to one could be an appealing option. But an independent birthing center located at a distance from a hospital could mean trouble in an emergency, such as one requiring a caesarean; it could necessitate something like a car-chase scene in a movie to get you to a hospital.

Another alternative site for delivery is your home. Some childbirth experts advocate home births, arguing that women are most likely to deliver naturally and easily if they're comfortable with their environment— and what could be more comfortable than home? But a decision to give birth at home should not be taken lightly—and it's dubious that it should be taken at all. Emergencies, such as those requiring caesareans, do happen, and there have been maternal and infant deaths in home deliveries that would have been avoided in a medical facility. Emergencies don't happen often, but I believe it's more of a risk than you should take.

CHAPTER 6

Avoiding a Caesarean: Your Role in Labor

Choosing a particular doctor and a particular hospital are decisions that may slightly tilt your odds of having a caesarean one way or the other. But these decisions are only the preliminaries. Often, it is what happens once labor is under way that determines which route your baby will travel to be born.

As we have emphasized throughout this book, there are instances in which a caesarean is the best alternative, and a woman who's enjoyed an uncomplicated pregnancy may yet run into trouble in the delivery room. Having a caesarean is not a sign of failure. Still, there are ways you can decrease the likelihood that you will need surgical assistance during childbirth.

PREPARE YOURSELF FOR LABOR

Generations ago, births were typically attended by midwives, along with other women and younger girls in the family. By the time a woman's turn to give birth came around, she was familiar with the physical ordeal of labor and the demands that would be placed on her. Today, the hospital has replaced the home as the site of childbirth, and aside from perhaps a simulation on film or a description in a book, many women go into pregnancy without the slightest idea of what labor will be like.

Although labor is a thoroughly natural process and much of the "work" you'll do instinctually, there are skills you need to learn to facilitate the process. For this reason, one of the best things you can do for yourself is to take a childbirth class. Most obstetricians and hospitals have a referral list, and many hospitals themselves offer classes. Both of the major childbirth methods (Lamaze and Bradley) have national organizations with local chapters, which you can contact if you'd like to study their approach. Then there's the International Childbirth Education Association, which can provide information on a number of different types of classes (see Chapter 8).

Which class is the best varies from place to place. Get recommendations from friends who have taken childbirth classes. Factors to consider include the class size, the fee, and where the classes are held. Many childbirth educators maintain that a class of more than fifteen couples is too large to afford much individual attention. On the other hand, one that consists of only a few couples offers little in the way of group feedback. Classes based at hospitals or other institutions tend to be larger, and they also may have greater access to visual aids and other facilities. Some private childbirth educators set up sessions with individual couples alone. To a great extent, your choice will depend on what you and the father, if he is to attend with you, feel most comfortable with.

Childbirth classes can be incredibly helpful in cae-sarean avoidance for several reasons. For one, the thought of labor, like any unknown quantity, can be quite intim-idating. The more you arm yourself with knowledge and skills beforehand, the more confident you will be going in. The same applies to the father. The more at ease with the process he is, the better able he'll be to offer support.

When labor draws near, being relaxed and assured clearly helps it along. Tension—which the classes help to minimize—can impede the dilation of the cervix. It can also slow down the pace of labor. While a long, arduous labor doesn't always mean that a caesarean is imminent, it can effectively sap your strength so that you all but run out of energy just when you need it.

A good preparation class will ensure that you're well versed in certain essential techniques, such as *pushing*. A lot of caesareans are done during the pushing phase, which occurs after the cervix has dilated fully. Some-times the baby comes down seemingly on its own, but pushing does add to the force. If the baby doesn't descend to a point where it can be delivered easily, a caesarean might have to be done. Pushing is best learned prior to labor; if you wait until you are in labor—learn-ing on the job, so to speak—the pain and other sensa-tions may be distracting and pushing may be less effective.

The proper breathing techniques are also quite im-portant to learn. They can be helpful not only in relax-ation but also in controlling pain. Thus, learned labor skills can lessen your need for medication. If you can keep the pain down to the tolerable range on your own, you're able to do with little or no medication. This is significant, for pain killers can sometimes diminish your resolve or the effectiveness of your pushing.

Even if you're planning a caesarean, it's advisable to take a childbirth class if there's the slightest chance that you'll go into labor. A breech baby, for example, may spontaneously turn around at a very late date. In this case, the skills you've learned will come in quite handy—even if only to get you to the hospital.

Even if you're quite set on a vaginal birth, do attend the class sessions on caesarean delivery. There's always a chance that you'll need one. If you're familiar with the operation and what it involves, you'll be better able to cope with it, should the need for it arise. Furthermore, you'll be better informed about the choices you have that could make the caesarean as close to a natural birth as possible.

BE REALISTIC ABOUT LABOR

Good preparation for labor includes preparing yourself not only for what you will do but for what you can expect. Anyone who leads you to believe that labor is the next best thing to a honeymoon or a Sunday stroll is not doing you a favor. Some labors are easier than others, but none are fun. This isn't to say that the very prospect should fill you with dread, but it's important to have some perspective on it. If you expect labor to be a breeze and it turns out not to be, you may feel too stunned and overwhelmed to cope with it effectively. If, on the other hand, you know that some labors drag on for twenty-four or even forty-eight hours, it may not be pleasant, but at least you'll know that what you're going through is normal.

The point is that labor varies from woman to woman. You can't always predict it, and it isn't always fair. Yours might be fast and easy, or it might be tedious and long. It may happen so fast that you won't have time to do the relaxing you've trained yourself to do, or it may go on for so long that you'll have a chance to get some sleep. Most labors are neither one nor the other but have ebbs and surges of various experiences and emotions within them. Labor is undeniably the great unknown that looms ahead of every expectant mother.

In our age, we're used to exerting a great deal of control over our lives. Certain aspects of our lives are planned and manipulable as never before. Simply the unknown nature of an upcoming labor, in such an era, can be quite foreboding in itself. But you have to accept that you'll have to go with your labor, no matter how it turns out.

UNDERSTAND YOUR OWN FEELINGS ABOUT LABOR

Childbirth is an incredibly physical process, in which your body expands—literally and figuratively—to new limits. But it also has a psychological component. Your state of mind and its acceptance of the physical changes and the processes that unfold can affect how the labor progresses, both negatively and positively.

Perhaps the most critical aspect of the mind-body connection with respect to labor is the "letting go." While giving birth, you let go in a number of ways: you let go of yourself as your body surrenders to the demands of labor; you let go of inhibitions—making noises, moving around; and you also let go of the child you've held within you for these several months.

The feeling of peace with your body and your impending motherhood can help you keep up with labor's powerful momentum. But other fears and emotions may serve to hold you back: distrust of labor, fear for your safety or that of the baby, uncertainty about motherhood, or discomfort about your sexuality. If your mind pulls back from the natural force of labor, your body is likely to withdraw as well. So your body might close down at the very time it should ideally be opening up.

During childbirth, you may feel quite emotional or vulnerable, and feelings usually kept safely hidden may rise to the surface. Sometimes childbirth raises feelings about other reproductive issues from your past, such as previous abortions, sexual abuse, or miscarriages. This can occur even if consciously you've left these memories behind. It can also stir up conflicts about your own parents, especially your relationship with your mother, and feelings that were instilled in you in childhood about childbirth and parenthood.

Also many women are uncomfortable about their bodies. For some, this results from previous physical or sexual experiences. For others, it reflects messages about femininity or sexuality received early in childhood. Beyond this, it's often socially derived. In our society, which values youth and thinness, many women come to feel that their bodies are "bad" if they fail to conform to the physical "ideal" we're bombarded with through the media and the movies. Studies consistently show that women are dissatisfied with their bodies and overestimate how "fat" they are, while men seem to view their bodies more realistically.

Such conflicts may give a woman the sense that she doesn't "deserve" a smooth labor and delivery. Guilt may play a role. If she once had an abortion, for example, she may feel that she needs to be "punished" for it. Or if she is ashamed of her body, she may not regard it as "good enough" to achieve a successful labor.

Case History: As her pregnancy neared term, it was so much on her mind that Denise felt she had to tell someone—and the someone she told was her doctor. She had become pregnant at the age of eighteen and had had an abortion at a local clinic. It had been a painful experience, both physically and emotionally. For months afterward, she had been terribly self-conscious, wondering whether other people knew about it or could somehow tell simply from looking at her. To this day, her husband was unaware of it, but as she approached bringing this new pregnancy to fruition, feelings about that early experience flooded back to her.

Her doctor advised Denise to see a counselor and to consider whether it would be appropriate to discuss it with her husband. It might be time to relieve herself from some of the pressure about a past event that, after all, she could do nothing about now. Before she got around to meeting with the counselor, however, Denise went into early labor. She felt quite tense and over-whelmed by pain during the contractions—whether this was in part due to her own fears and memories, neither she nor her doctor knew for sure. But an epidural allowed her to relax and continue through to delivery.

Because all these feelings can intrude on your ability to submit wholly to labor, it is helpful to explore them ahead of time. If recollections of certain painful experiences arise during your pregnancy, discuss them with your doctor, your childbirth instructor, or a therapist. If you feel comfortable raising them in front of others or think that others may share them, bring them up at your childbirth class. It can be very reassuring to realize that you're not alone in your experience or insecurities. Recognizing this can enhance your own sense of strength and confidence.

Counseling and support can help you feel good about your body—which is how you should feel. Your body has the power to create life, which is something to celebrate, not to withdraw from.

STAY IN TOUCH WITH WHAT YOUR BODY NEEDS

In the United States, we have a rather odd custom with regard to childbirth. The mother is expected to lie on her back, passively, with her feet possibly bound by stirrups. Exactly how this custom developed is not clear; perhaps it made it easier for a physician to tend to many laboring women. Or perhaps its origin is psychological, in that it could reflect men's (the doctors') fears about women being out of control. In this interpretation, men limited women's movements and discouraged their spontaneity, ensuring that they remained docile, quiet, and utterly nonthreatening, in order that they—the men—maintain their own sense of power in the situation.

Whatever its origin, it is clear that a supine position is the least viable position in which to labor. Especially in the early stages, labor is overwhelmingly an active process, and this position is not one that encourages great activity or mobility. The supine position may lower blood pressure, which could lead to fetal distress. It may allow little leverage for pushing. The contractions may be less forceful, yet more painful. In many cases, especially in early labor, the lying-on-the-back position tends to slow labor down.

Fortunately, this is changing to some extent. But the idea still persists that going into labor means taking to bed. At some point you will probably want to take to your bed; you may feel exhausted and need a rest, or lying down may seem to be the most comfortable position at a particular time. But in early labor, it is undoubtedly better to try to keep active and upright.

The fact is that moving around and shifting position can aid in labor. Getting off your back relieves the pressure on the main blood vessel to the uterus, so there's no restricted blood flow. It can ease discomfort and speed up the process. It helps you feel more in control of what's happening.

Your guide to what to do is what you *feel* you want to do. Trust what your body is telling you. Some women find walking most helpful. Others feel better sitting in a low chair.

In early labor, your movements should in no way be constricted, either physically or by your own sense of appropriateness. In early labor, ask if you can be monitored externally and be unhooked to move around. As you stroll, your partner can walk with you or stay nearby so you have someone to lean on as your contractions are occurring.

With all the strain and exertion of labor, you're bound to get hungry and thirsty. To some medical minds, the intravenous is the answer, but eating and drinking lightly are options in early labor. In the past, eating during labor was forbidden because of the risk of aspirating stomach contents, should the mother need anesthesia. But the real risk is not the food being digested but the gastric acids that the stomach produces when no food is present. The field of anesthesiology has so advanced that the risks of fatal choking and aspiration into the lungs have dropped to near nil. If your physician has told you that you are at high risk for a caesarean section, however, it may be safer not to eat during labor. In this case, discuss it with your physician.

This is not to imply that you should sit down to a hearty meal—but then again, it's doubtful you'll want to. Fruit juices, soup, and toast are more likely to constitute the menu of choice. Again, what's important is that you attend to your own needs. Would a competitive athlete enter a long tournament on a regimen of ice chips? Know that your own private marathon will require some reserves, and sustain your energy level accordingly.

It's a good idea to empty your bladder frequently. As labor goes on, you might not even notice that you need to urinate because your mind will be caught up with your contractions and because pressure on or damage to the nerves in your bladder might keep you from physically feeling it. But a full bladder can interfere with the baby's descent. Urine sometimes seeps out anyway during vigorous pushing, but try to remember to go to the bathroom every hour or two, or have someone remind you to. If the bladder doesn't appear to be fully emptying—a not uncommon occurrence—a catheter might be needed.

During labor, do not only stay aware of your needs but express those needs to others as well. No one is going to guess what is concerning you. If you're bothered by noise or interruptions, speak up. If you need more pillows, ask. Your labor support person, your partner, or whoever else you have chosen can act as an intermediary to follow through with your requests.

BE REALISTIC ABOUT MEDICATION

As a rule, it's best to avoid taking medication if possible—it can disrupt labor in a variety of ways. The physical effects of a medicine can halt progress, and even just the awareness of a further intrusion can break the momentum. An epidural during labor can alter your sensations so that your pushing impulse is dimmed. Demerol (a common pain medication) can interfere with your ability to concentrate and focus on breathing techniques.

On the other hand, such medications do have their place. If you're in severe pain, you're not going to be terribly effective at pushing, and your discomfort may simply overwhelm your resolve. If you've endured as much as you can and feel ready to take medication, you don't have to feel that you've "given in." You've simply taken the best route for your particular labor. Pain leaves some women tense and their cervix rigid. Sometimes an epidural is all they need to relax their bodies and reach full dilation.

If you've done your groundwork and selected a doctor who shares your views, you should be able to trust that doctor's recommendations concerning medication. Only if you haven't worked out these issues beforehand might you feel you're waging a personal war that pits your desire for relief against your distrust of medication.

DON'T GO TO THE HOSPITAL TOO EARLY

Sometimes the membranes rupture early, before full-fledged labor begins, but the expectant mother goes to the hospital on her initial impulse. The clock immediately starts ticking. She fails to deliver within a set time and finds herself heading for surgery.

The main reason for urgency with ruptured membranes is that they make you more vulnerable to infection. But the hospital environment probably harbors more sources of infection, and you may be better off at home until labor begins in earnest. Alert your doctor as to what has happened, however. Unless you have some risk factors that may require monitoring, in early labor it is probably a good idea to stay someplace that's comfortable and familiar, if your doctor agrees.

At what point should you venture off to the hospital? This can require guesswork. Some childbirth experts say that intense contractions with only a few moments' break between them signal that it's time to make the trip.

This is something you should discuss with your doctor ahead of time. Certain physicians have their own policies. Some prefer that you be in the hospital where you can be watched; others feel that you should be admitted only after a certain amount of time. In some facilities, you can go and be checked without having to check in. At New York Hospital, for example, expectant mothers can come in for an examination, be monitored for fifteen minutes, then walk around without going to the labor floor. They may even go home if it's quite early. If you go elsewhere during the daytime, you might be able to stop in at your doctor's office for a brief examination.

Much depends on how far you live from the hospital and where your doctor is located. If you live a full hour away, for instance, rather than running out there and then back a few times, you might prefer to get settled in at the hospital.

Case History: Pregnant with her first child, Shari was having mild contractions every fifteen minutes or so and wasn't quite sure what they meant. She hadn't slept very well the night before, partly because of her apprehension, and wanted to make sure everything was okay and that there was nothing more she should be doing. Her husband drove her to the doctor, who told them that she hadn't dilated at all, so the only thing for her to do was wait. Wait! This is not an easy task when something tremendous is about to happen and you don't know what to expect.

So Shari and her husband did just what they usually do when they have a few hours to pass in town: they went to the movies. Since it was the noon show, the place was just about empty—making it all the easier for Shari to really stretch out and be comfortable. After the movie, she was rechecked. Little had progressed, so they went back home. In the middle of the night, real labor began. They dressed, grabbed keys and Shari's suitcase, and headed for the hospital. Only then did Shari realize how different her earlier mild cramps had been from the real thing.

Some women actually conceal their active labors to avoid going to the hospital for fear of increasing their risk of having a caesarean. Be reasonable about this. If you're at a point where you can't walk or stand up comfortably, you're doing yourself no service by remaining at home. Labor doesn't always start predictably, and some labors begin in full force without any apparent early stages.

DON'T NEGATIVELY AFFECT LABOR

Fact: Your chances of having a caesarean rise dramatically if you demand a caesarean during labor. There might be moments when you feel you just can't take it anymore, and the thought of letting the doctor do the rest seems eminently appealing.

Shouting "I give up" or declaring that you want surgery should not affect the doctor's judgment of what is truly best for you, but of course it does. No physician wants to see a patient suffer. In a case like this, a doctor who is vacillating between sticking it out with a long labor or resorting to a caesarean may start leaning toward the latter.

It's not that women should be martyrs to childbirth, but sometimes they may unwittingly tip a doctor's judgment in the direction of surgical delivery. Your saying you want the pain to end may really be a request for emotional support to get you through, but it may be interpreted as a plea for a caesarean section. Don't forget that those surrounding you are trained to use the tools that they have at their disposal—namely, a host of medications and medical apparatus. Once you start calling for help, that's the particular brand of help they're likely to give.

Being knowledgeable about the labor process can help. The final stage of active labor, when the cervix dilates rapidly, is often the part women find most uncomfortable. But it's also one of the briefest, sometimes lasting only forty-five minutes or less. If you have an idea of what's happening, the knowledge that the pain will soon abate can help you endure it.

Doctors have seen many patients react similarly, and they know that it will pass quickly. But your husband may not know this. It can be terribly frightening for a man to watch someone he loves struggle so, and he might start pressuring the doctor to do something. It's essential that the father or anyone else attending the birth have an understanding of the birth process and know what to expect.

When things get difficult, you do have to rely on your internal strength to some extent. Recognize what your support people can and cannot do. They can offer encouragement, but they cannot take your pain away.

For their support to help, you have to be receptive to it. If you've already decided in your own mind that you've had more than you can take, their kind words will fall on your deaf ears, and you could be on your way to a caesarean.

CHAPTER 7

Risks and
Aftereffects

In undergoing a caesarean delivery or any other operation, you're subjecting yourself to a degree of risk. What's unique to caesareans, however, is that it's not you alone but your child as well who's exposed to the risk of complications from surgery. Improvements in both technique and technology have made caesareans much safer than they have ever been. But medical control and predictability come at some potential cost. All other factors being equal, the risks of a caesarean are far greater than those of a vaginal birth. Of course, you rarely consider risks by themselves. You generally weigh the risks of a vaginal delivery that could be traumatic to you and/or your child against the increased risk of the caesarean operation.

The complications that occur are usually quite minor and easily correctable. But some postsurgical problems may require additional surgery or treatment. The more serious the problem that originally necessitated the surgical delivery, the more likely it is that complications will arise. Although the overwhelming likelihood is that you'll emerge from your caesarean and recovery feeling every bit yourself, it's essential that you remain aware of the hazards as you consider your birthing options—particularly since those associated with vaginal delivery are much lower.

THE RISKS OF CAESAREANS

The first risk to note is the mortality rate for caesarean births—the risk of death. There is one maternal death for every 2,500 to 5,000 caesarean deliveries. This rate is two to four times the mortality rate for vaginal births. It should be noted that many of the women who undergo caesareans are at high risk to begin with—as sufferers of diabetes or heart disease, for example; so the elevated mortality rate cannot be attributed to the caesarean alone.

Among low-risk caesarean births, such as elective repeat caesareans, the figures are on the low end—about one death per five thousand births. But since the low risk still exceeds the risk of vaginal delivery, the decision to have a caesarean should not be taken lightly.

Death may result from rare complications that can arise during the operation (acute infection, hemorrhaging, extreme reaction to anesthesia) or from conditions that existed previously (such as cardiac or pulmonary disease). Even so, the mortality rate is relatively low, so if you do have a caesarean, the odds are very much in your favor.

Here are some of the most typical complications that follow from a caesarean. Only a small number of women get them. They are not totally preventable, and you can never say that beyond a doubt they will not crop up. But you can minimize the likelihood that they will arise by taking proper care of yourself throughout pregnancy and by having a highly skilled physician who is well versed in good surgical techniques.

Infection

Caesareans present a greater risk of infection, either in the uterus or at the site of incision, than vaginal births. Uterine infection, most often called *endometritis*, can occur in either a caesarean or a vaginal delivery. For caesarean mothers, they're most common during emergency deliveries after a long labor. In fact, the longer the labor goes on after the membranes have ruptured, the more prone the mother will be to infection. This is because bacteria from the vagina can make their way up to the uterine cavity and cause infection. For this reason, frequent vaginal exams during labor can be a factor in infection.

An infection can prolong a mother's sojourn in the hospital, but it's rarely a serious problem. It can usually be treated successfully and rapidly with antibiotics. Many physicians now administer antibiotics at the time of surgery as a preventive measure. This can lower the incidence of infection, although it does not always prevent them.

Infections are often detected and treated during the hospital stay, but it's possible that one could develop later. If you get a fever or notice a foul-smelling discharge from the vagina or from the area of incision, contact your doctor immediately.

Bleeding

As one obstetrics and gynecology textbook puts it, "Caesarean section is not a blood-conserving procedure." Some blood loss—at least one pint—is to be expected, and there's a risk that the loss could become significant. Hemorrhage can also occur after a vaginal birth, but the likelihood is much greater with a caesarean, and even without complications, the blood loss is about twice as much.

Excessive bleeding can result if the incision in the uterus extends into the uterine vessels during surgery. It can also result if the incision must be extended to accommodate a large or awkwardly positioned infant. Finally, bleeding problems can occur if the uterus fails to contract immediately after the placenta has been removed. If the hemorrhaging is severe, the blood vessels at the uterus can sometimes be tied off, but in rare cases a hysterectomy proves necessary.

Some caesarean mothers lose enough blood to require a transfusion. Check with your doctor to see if there's any reason for you to anticipate needing a transfusion and to discuss any options you might have in preparation for this. For minor blood loss, which is more common, additional iron supplements are generally all that's necessary.

Postoperative Pulmonary Problems

Sometimes a condition called *postoperative atelectasis* (limited air in the lungs) develops in the period after a caesarean delivery. In this condition, the lungs do not expand fully. This happens partly because the anesthetic tends to slow down all your systems and partly because, like many postoperative patients, caesarean mothers breathe shallowly to avoid the abdominal pain that deep breathing may cause. Many are reluctant to breathe deeply or cough for fear that the incision will open.

Be assured that this will not happen. Try shifting your position or holding a pillow or a towel against your abdomen when you cough.

It's important that you work on your breathing, even if it hurts at first. Get yourself back to breathing normally by taking deep breaths—and even by coughing—as soon after surgery as you are able. The nurses on staff should be able to assist you. The more you do it, the faster your discomfort will fade—and the sooner you'll be able to focus more energy on your baby.

Some women, especially those who have chronic respiratory ailments, may need additional help, such as an oxygen mask with built-in pressure.

One way to guard against this problem is to be in good aerobic health—and to not smoke. If the operation is strictly an elective procedure, it might not be advisable to have it if a respiratory infection is present.

Anesthetic Complications

In the past, anesthesia presented a high risk during caesareans. Today, the advancement and control of anesthetic techniques have made acute and dangerous reactions quite rare. But some people do react severely to general anesthesia. If you've had complications from anesthesia before—or if any relative has, as this tendency may run in families—be sure to tell your doctor.

Regional anesthetics are less likely to cause serious problems. But if you have any fears about the anesthetic, raise them with a professional. For many, the notion of being "out" and not in control can be frightening in itself, especially if they've never had an anesthetic before. The doctor should be able to allay any fears and to determine which anesthetic is the most appropriate for you. With regional anesthesia (spinal or epidural) a small percentage of patients experience severe headaches after surgery.

Injury to Other Pelvic Organs

In rare instances, a caesarean results in injury to adjacent organs in the pelvic cavity, such as the bladder or intestines. For the low transverse incision generally used today, the bladder must be pushed down during the operation. This may cause a bladder injury, particularly because the bladder tends to be drawn up high due to the forces of labor. Accidents are also more likely to occur if adhesions from previous pelvic surgery (such as a previous caesarean or a myomectomy, to remove fibroids) are present. A loop of bowel, for example, may adhere to a previous incision. Injury to the bladder is most frequent after repeat caesareans, but even so, the rate is less than one percent.

An injury to the urinary or gastrointestinal tract is usually recognized and attended to immediately. Such an occurrence might prolong recuperation time but should not lead to any long-term complications. If an injury is not discovered or if its symptoms do not arise until later, the treatment is a bit more complex and is dealt with on an individual basis.

Bladder or Bowel Discomfort

Some women experience mild urinary difficulties as a result of their bladder becoming overdistended during labor or after surgery. This can happen if the bladder is not emptied frequently before the operation. Temporary damage to the nerves of the bladder may result, which can impair your ability to sense whether your bladder is full. This is treated simply by using a catheter for a few days.

If this happens to you, try to urinate on your own after the catheter is removed. If you find yourself unable to urinate every four hours or so, let the doctor or nurse know. Similarly, alert someone to any burning, urgency, or other discomfort so that a culture can be taken to test for a possible infection.

After any abdominal operation, temporary paralysis of the bowel is a frequent complaint. A sluggish bowel can cause cramps or bloating, but though uncomfortable, neither is serious. Either can result from not eating, from the relaxing effects of an anesthetic (especially a general) or subsequent pain killers, or from digestive disorientation from being in a strange place or eating on a different schedule. A gradual return to a normal diet is usually all the treatment that's done, and the discomfort should ease within a few days.

Abnormal Clotting

A *thrombosis*, or blood clot, sometimes develops as a complication of surgery, and it may threaten to partially or completely block off a blood vessel, especially in the legs. Clotting is most likely to develop after a period of immobility, when your blood flow has grown sluggish.

Women at the highest risk of having a dangerous clot include those who smoke or are overweight. Thromboses sometimes develop among women who deliver vaginally, but are about ten times more common among caesarean mothers.

Clots tend to form in the lower half of the body, but they may travel to the lungs (where they are termed *pulmonary embolisms*). Early symptoms are swelling in the leg or ankle, soreness on movement, and tenderness in midcalf. If the problem occurs in the lungs, you might get pain upon breathing or a dry cough.

If you develop any of these symptoms, let your physician know. Prompt treatment of an abnormal blood clot can prevent life-threatening complications.

EMOTIONAL AFTEREFFECTS

The aftermath of a caesarean brings the same emotional aftereffects that vaginal birth does—complicated by the addition of emotions and physical responses related specifically to the operation itself. It is a complex matter because there are so many individual responses and sources of responses.

The emotional aftermath of any pregnancy produces physical responses. Hormonal changes can prompt depression, so a new mother may experience mood shifts. In addition, the extreme fatigue caused by surgery may leave a caesarean mother feeling helpless, frustrated, or depressed at a time when she wants to devote her energy to her child.

Moreover, it is not uncommon for a caesarean mother

to be plagued with feelings of anger or self-doubt that seem to arise from the operation itself. Some women feel themselves to be failures because they were unable to give birth "normally." Others may feel angry or deprived, believing that an important experience to which they were entitled had been taken away from them.

Case History: About a month after Ronnie's caesarean, the new-baby visits and the phone calls simmered down and she began to feel low. She was thrilled with her new son and she was working at home part time, but something still felt unsettled.

On her physician's advice, Ronnie had had a planned caesarean because she periodically suffered from herpes. But now she regretted that she hadn't questioned his advice. Most of her new-mother friends had gone through labor or at least had taken childbirth classes, and it seemed to Ronnie as if she had delivered her baby the way one brings in an appliance for repairs—with everything scheduled and plotted out ahead of time.

In retrospect, she understood that she had felt threatened by the labor process and had failed to deal with her own uncertainties and ambivalences. So at the time, she had welcomed the doctor's suggestion with relief rather than skepticism.

Her little boy suffered from a clubfoot, and Ronnie couldn't help but feel that maybe the surgery had been a factor, even though she knew it was irrational to think so.

Emotional issues affect a person on both the conscious and the unconscious levels. Consciously, a woman may be relieved that she didn't have to go through a difficult labor, but unconsciously, she may feel somehow incomplete because she did not pass what she perceived to be a test. She may never articulate these unconscious feelings, even to herself, but she may become depressed if she fails to resolve them. Similarly, a woman may consciously be grateful to her physician for delivering an intact baby, but somewhere underneath it all, she may be furious at him or her for putting her through surgery.

Any of several causes can bring about the anger. A caesarean mother might be angry at herself for "letting" it happen to her and her baby. She might be angry at her husband for not doing enough or for not fully appreciating what she's gone through. She might even feel angry at the baby for coming down in the "wrong" position or coming down slowly and causing her all this trouble.

Because many of us have grown up feeling that it's not appropriately feminine behavior to express anger, women commonly repress angry emotions. Suppressed anger is sometimes turned inward and experienced as depression. A woman's feeling that she lacks control can also cause a depressed state. Many women feel powerless over their bodies after having a caesarean; they view it as something that happened to them without their planning it, and they may feel helpless as a result.

A caesarean may stir up a woman's feelings about her sexual history or her upbringing. As they often do during pregnancy, previously hidden conflicts about an abortion, a miscarriage, or a rape, or ambivalence about motherhood may come to the surface after a caesarean.

Often a subsequent pregnancy brings out into the open an emotional reaction to a previous caesarean that the woman hardly knew was there. She may seem to have had no problem with the first caesarean, but as the labor date approaches, she may become anxious and troubled by memories and dreams of her operation. She could dread "failing" yet another time, or fear being at the mercy of doctors again. If such feelings do emerge, discuss them with your doctor or another professional.

The women most prone to postcaesarean depression are those who during pregnancy were most determined not to have one. Women whose unquestioned priority was having a healthy baby tend not to be as troubled. The key is to take a realistic view during pregnancy. A woman who accepts that a caesarean could be the best thing for her baby regards it as an assurance gained rather than as anything lost. But if having a caesarean thrusts her into the role of a "sick" person rather than that of healthy new mother, she may suffer in self-esteem.

The vast majority of caesarean mothers do not have severe emotional responses to their deliveries. Most are far too enthralled—and busy—with their new infants to dwell on the discomforts of the operation. Any woman who does experience emotional consequences should bring them up with her doctor. Often simply understanding why the caesarean was necessary can help her place it in perspective. If the problem has deeper psychological roots, some form of therapy might be preferable. Caesarean support groups (see Chapter 8) can also help pull a woman out of her postcaesarean blues.

The father, too, might react to a caesarean with anger, confusion, and disappointment. He might feel guilty, as if the entire ordeal were his fault, or he could be plagued by a sense that his partner let him down. Both parents need to be open and willing to discuss these issues—with a professional, if necessary—since they can affect how you relate to each other and to your child.

Sexuality

Many women experience changes in their sexuality after having a baby. A good part of this has to do with a new mother's schedule; free time and physical vigor are scarce resources when there's a newborn baby in the house. The change may also result from her shifting hormonal levels.

After a delivery, most doctors suggest waiting two to six weeks before resuming sexual intercourse. In the postbirth period, sex might be mildly uncomfortable, since the vagina may not stretch or lubricate sufficiently. More changes probably result from a vaginal delivery, but they can occur after a caesarean as well. If sex does prove uncomfortable or painful, tell your doctor. Sometimes a lubricating jelly is all you need.

Aside from bodily changes, anything that touches you emotionally can also affect your sexuality. Because of their change in life-style, self-perception, and body image after a birth, many new mothers and fathers must get reacquainted sexually. This can happen after any kind of birth, but some feelings may be particular to caesareans. If a woman feels less feminine because she didn't labor, her sense of her own sexuality might be altered as well. Likewise, a man might be reluctant to impregnate his wife again if he feels that he is to blame for her surgery. Be forthright about these feelings, and reassure each other where emotions are raw.

If the feelings persist, you may want to consider counseling.

Under ordinary circumstances, there's no reason for a caesarean to compromise a woman's future prospects for having babies. Only the rare case of a severe infection would have a strong negative impact on fertility. A buildup of scar tissue in the pelvic cavity, particularly after several caesareans, can have some effect as well.

Some women want to get pregnant immediately after their child is born. Many doctors feel that if the first birth is a caesarean, it's best to wait six months before conceiving again and again launching into the physical stresses and changes of pregnancy, to give the body a rest. Some experts urge the same period of waiting after a vaginal delivery. If you wish to conceive again shortly after your caesarean, discuss it with your doctor. It is probably a good idea to take iron and vitamin supplements to build up your blood supply in the meantime.

Bonding

A caesarean may interfere with the bonding process between mother and child. Much has been made of the fact that early bonding—the close attachment formed by mother-infant contact during the initial hours of life—seems to be important to the mother-child relationship. After a caesarean, the mother might not get to see her baby immediately after the birth because of anesthesia or sedation. For the next day or so, she may be medicated or in pain, or the baby may require medical treatment, or hospital policy may preclude their being together. Even when they are together, the mother may have a tougher time focusing on her infant because she's trying to recover from and resolve the entire experience in her mind. And in some cases, negative feelings about the form of delivery can color the mother's feelings about the infant.

It's not clear exactly why bonding is significant, but research suggests that it does affect a woman's self-confidence as a mother and her acceptance of a child. A caesarean needn't intrude on the process very severely. First of all, many hospitals allow a mother to stay awake and hold her baby while she gets stitched up during the operation. If you're not feeling up to caring for your infant for the first few days, allow the nurse to do the routine care; you just let the baby snuggle with you in bed. Don't feel guilty if you need a night or so of sleep.

If you do feel well enough, make an effort to spend time with your baby. But despite all good intentions, you may not feel ready to care totally for the baby so soon after surgery. Keep in mind that it's not all or nothing—it's not that either you're the "good" mother and do everything for the baby or you do nothing at all. While you're in the hospital, you can have the baby with you while you rest and have a nurse take care of the baby's needs. If you're still actively recuperating when you get home, do some tasks for the baby while a relative or someone else does the cooking or other chores around the house.

Don't forget the father—let him take up some of the slack. The word you hear today is not *mothering* but *parenting*. A man can change diapers as well as you can. Because it may be a struggle for you to take care of the baby in the first few weeks, explore the possibility of his taking time off. Some companies today offer paternal leave with part or full pay.

Case History: A few months ago, Jill had her fourth child, a daughter, by caesarean. Recently remarried, this was her new husband Tom's first baby. Unlike Jill, Tom runs his own business and is much more flexible in how much time he could take from work. So when Jill went back to her job as soon as she was able, Tom made it a priority to care for their baby.

"I have to admit that for a time I was jealous that he got the chance to get close to the baby—especially when she seemed to recognize him quicker than me," she reflects. "But when I saw how much they enjoyed each other, I was really just happy about it. Now that our lives are settling down a bit, I've been spending more time with the baby, and things are evening out. But I can't help noting that they do seem to share a special closeness that even our friends notice."

The increased paternal involvement that a caesarean demands is definitely a plus. Research shows that fathers of caesarean babies spend more time with their infants, tend to soothe and talk to them more, and overall feel more positively about them. Such a good beginning can pave the way to an enhanced relationship between father and child.

EFFECTS ON THE BABY

The effects of a caesarean delivery on the baby are a tricky issue, because if the baby suffers any ill effects of delivery, it's hard to know exactly what to attribute it to. If a mother has a caesarean because her baby is high risk and something ultimately does go awry, it's likely that the original condition—and not the caesarean—was a major factor. Breech babies, for instance, have a greater risk of complications at birth, regardless of the mode of delivery. So a breech baby delivered by caesarean that does have difficulties at birth may still be better off than he or she would have been had a vaginal birth been attempted. Moreover, a great many premature babies are delivered by caesarean. Any complications they suffer may be due to the prematurity and not to the operation itself.

A baby that arrives by caesarean has skipped the journey down the birth canal. Caesarean babies tend to look quite peaceful and pretty at birth because they've had no molding or bruising from being squeezed through the birth passage. But they also miss some of the positive aspects of the mother's labor; for example, the journey through the mother's body seems to play a role in preparing the baby's lungs for breathing independently.

Overall, your baby should not suffer from having had an abdominal birth. However, as in a vaginal birth, in a caesarean there's always a risk that not all will go as planned. Here are some possible risks that you should be aware of:

• The surgeon can accidentally cut the baby when opening up the uterine wall. If the baby has descended head first, the surgeon might do this on its scalp or face. In the rare instances when this occurs, it's normally just a scratch, but stitches might be necessary to ensure proper healing.

• Although in such cases a caesarean is often considered easier on the baby, an exceptionally large or difficultly positioned infant is at a greater risk of sustaining an injury at birth. For example, with a breech baby the shoulders are prone to injury, regardless of birth method.

• The baby might have initial breathing difficulties if mucus or other secretions haven't been squeezed out during the passage through the birth canal. Moreover, if a caesarean baby takes a deep breath, whatever is in its pharynx might go into its lungs. To counteract any problems, the contents of the baby's mouth and throat are suctioned. This may prove necessary with some infants delivered vaginally as well.

• If an elective caesarean is done before the mother spontaneously goes into labor, the baby might not yet be ready to be born, most notably because the respiratory system may be immature. This usually results from a miscalculation in the baby's age. Today, tests for fetal age—including sonography early in the pregnancy and amniocentesis to test for lung maturity—can be done that minimize the chances that this will happen.

• Sometimes a baby must be delivered prematurely, if complications of pregnancy occur. Such a baby will probably need to be placed in the premature intensive care unit and could require supplementary oxygen or a respirator.

• An infant suffering from respiratory distress syndrome, in which the lungs are not fully mature, may be vulnerable to the secondary problems that premature infants suffer, such as pneumonia or seizures. These complications may require a prolonged hospital stay.

• Certain maternal conditions leading up to a caesarean can contribute to a baby's difficulties at birth. Infants of diabetic mothers, for example, may suffer from extremely low blood sugar upon delivery and require special treatment.

• Any anesthesia or pain medication you take during pregnancy and labor crosses the placenta. Because of what it's absorbed, a newborn baby can appear depressed or slightly sluggish. This response is short-lived, however, and after respiratory assistance, there seem to be no long-term effects.

This sluggishness can occur regardless of how the baby is delivered. In fact, a long, heavily medicated vaginal birth can slow a baby's respiratory response more than a smooth caesarean delivery would. When general anesthesia is used, for example, the baby is exposed to the medication for no more than five minutes. Because of the potential effects, however, it's best not to take any more medication than you truly need.

• Just as the medication a pregnant woman takes enters the fetus's blood supply, the medication a nursing mother takes enters the newborn's milk supply. This is usually not of concern, although it's best to keep your medication down to a minimum. Complex medical problems requiring a lot of drugs should be discussed with your doctor. In some cases, breastfeeding is not possible while the mother is taking certain drugs.

After a caesarean, breast milk may take a day or so to get started, but this is no cause for worry.

As for long-term effects, there's little evidence for any differences between vaginal and caesarean delivery. Your caesarean-born child is no more or less fragile than a child born vaginally. Even though the beginning may not be as planned, your baby has every reason to expect vigorous growth and health.

CHAPTER 8

Making the Best of the Birth

A woman who has had a caesarean delivery should not feel as if something has been taken away from her. Her overwhelming sense should be that she has gained something—namely, the birth of a healthy baby. If the mother firmly believes that having the caesarean was the best and safest way to deliver her child, she will probably be at peace with it.

But if the caesarean mother looks back upon her operation with profound regret or anger, it's likely that something is amiss. If she's plagued by doubts that the surgery resulted from some weakness on her or her doctor's part, she may harbor ill feelings for quite a while. It's generally uncertainty that will haunt her for months or even years afterward.

Similarly, if a woman regards a natural delivery as a "good" birth and a caesarean as a "bad" one, an unplanned caesarean will leave her greatly disappointed. This is particularly the case if she has read and learned about and prepared herself mentally for a vaginal birth without realistically addressing the possibility that a caesarean might prove necessary for her.

But there's no reason for unpreparedness. If the caesarean is planned, there is ample time to get a second opinion, explore other delivery options, and gather all the information you need from your doctor or any other sources. You should not feel *pressured* to put your name on the schedule for surgery. If the caesarean is unplanned, you should have sufficient trust that your doctor will choose the best course for you and your baby. And even in an "emergency" caesarean, there's often still sufficient time to weigh the various treatment options and to consult a second physician. (If it's a true medical crisis and surgery cannot be delayed, then of course concern for your and your baby's safety takes precedence.) In any event, you should establish your priorities and contingency plans in advance so that if a caesarean is performed, you are confident that the circumstances demanded it and feel comfortable with how it proceeded.

A COOPERATIVE RELATIONSHIP WITH YOUR DOCTOR

In other words, a decision to have a caesarean should always be made in cooperation with your doctor, not in spite of your doctor and certainly not in complete deference to your doctor. In the case of an unplanned caesarean, your childbirth goals should be spelled out so that this rule applies here as well. Your relationship with your doctor must be a cooperative one from the start, not an adversarial one and not a passive one.

Having a doctor does not mean that you turn over complete responsibility for your health to another person. Sometimes we're tempted to put ourselves in a doctor's hands and let him or her take care of everything. This can be particularly easy to do during pregnancy, when you're feeling vulnerable and the thought of confronting a physician can be quite intimidating. But playing an active part in making decisions about your childbirth is ultimately empowering to you as a patient. Understanding what awaits you will relieve you from fearful anticipation and reduce the stress that goes along with both surgery and childbirth. Several studies have concluded that when people feel powerless and at the mercy of others, their ability to recuperate from illness or surgery is compromised. By being informed and confident of the decisions you make about childbirth, you're putting yourself in a position of strength.

It's often helpful for your husband to play a part right from the beginning. You, your husband, and your doctor are working together toward a common goal—the successful birth of your child—and it's essential that he feel as comfortable with the doctor as you do. He should be involved in making decisions as well as in becoming informed about childbirth alternatives. If he attends an office visit (or visits) with you, you're likely to feel more at ease. And it's easier to discuss the various issues with him afterward.

Case History: Erica and John were expecting their second child after recently moving to a new community. They decided that this time, John would be more involved in the birth than he had been the first time. After their first prenatal visit together, John said he didn't have a great feeling about the doctor. "He rushed us," he said, "and he seemed to barely pay attention to what you were saying about your previous pregnancy." "But he's supposed to be good," Erica protested. "Look at how crowded the waiting room was."

At her husband's urging, Erica did some checking and found that her chosen doctor, who had been recommended to her by a neighbor, had an exceedingly high caesarean rate. She learned that some women had complained that he had signed them out to other physicians without letting them know ahead of time, perhaps because he had overextended his practice. One physician's name kept coming up as an alternative, and the couple consulted with her. This doctor explained exactly how she worked with her two partners and spent some time answering questions. Erica and John left with a warmer, more secure feeling.

As a patient and as a pregnant woman, you have a number of rights. (See the Pregnant Patient's Bill of Rights, from the International Childbirth Education Association, Appendix B.)

FINANCIAL COSTS OF THE OPERATION

Remaining aware of these rights is essential as you deal with your physician. Many women seem to forget that their relationship with their obstetrician is based on the fact that he or she is providing a service. Women who demand promptness, fairness, and respect from any other professional without question often shy away from "troubling" their obstetricians with complaints or concerns. But it is your doctor's job to address matters of your pregnancy and impending delivery. Your health and comfort should be important to your doctor, and it should be important enough to you that you make certain that you get the best care.

Financial arrangements must be discussed up front as well. Many women are reluctant to raise money issues, because they fear it puts them in a bad light or because they're not comfortable dealing with money matters in general. You should not make important decisions regarding your pregnancy strictly on the basis of cost, but you do need to have a sense of how your treatment will affect you financially and what your financial options are.

Early on, you should discuss with your physician what the fee will be. Some doctors have the same fee for caesareans and vaginal births; others charge more for caesareans. Then check with your insurance company to see how the coverage works. The coverage may be greater for a caesarean, particularly in terms of the hospital stay (see Figure 9). Look farther than the dollars and cents—some insurance companies require you to see a doctor on their list or to attend a certain hospital. You should evaluate caregivers affiliated with your insurance firm every bit as carefully as anyone else. The doctor your insurance company recommends might have a high caesarean rate. Is the increased risk of surgery worth their coverage? Sometimes they offer partial reimbursement if you see a physician of your choice. It's up to you to check.

The earlier you look into insurance policies, the better. In fact, it can be financially disastrous to wait until you find yourself pregnant before applying for insurance. Today, when insurance companies are struggling to remain profit-making machines, a "preexisting" condition (such as pregnancy, if you apply while you're already expecting) will often not be covered. You may

Figure 9

Mean Length of Hospital Stay, by Type of Delivery, 1987

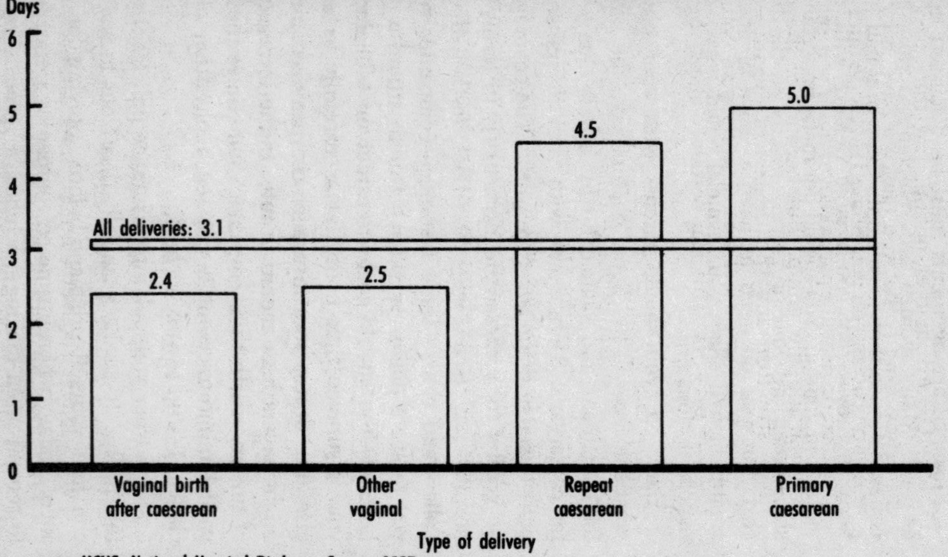

Days

All deliveries: 3.1

Vaginal birth after caesarean	2.4
Other vaginal	2.5
Repeat caesarean	4.5
Primary caesarean	5.0

Type of delivery

SOURCE: NCHS, National Hospital Discharge Survey, 1987

be covered by your spouse's policy, depending on what kind of plan he's on.

HMOs are another option, but they, too, present problems. One is that you may not have any say about which physician you get. Some HMOs do offer a degree of choice or provide partial coverage if you see a physician outside the group. But because of the organizational structure and the degree of incentives, HMO doctors sometimes feel less of a personal commitment to their patients. This can certainly affect the level of care.

This does not mean that you can't get excellent treatment from HMO-affiliated physicians. Under such circumstances, however, the more informed you are, the better. Ask questions and show interest. This will encourage your physician's own involvement. And if you truly do have questions about the care you're receiving or about the recommendations made to you, get an outside consultation—even if it means paying for it—to make sure that you're on the right track.

If you work, find out if your employee benefits contribute in any way. Some employers make provisions other than the standard health insurance to cover additional expenses. Check to see what you get in the way of disability or pregnancy leave, or whether your husband has the option of paternity leave. Some companies give a new mother or father a certain amount of time with pay or reduced pay. Because a caesarean can require a longer recovery, buying time can be that much more critical for both of you. Getting additional help at home is another possible cost, but this is generally not covered by insurance.

If the cost of the operation remains a problem, be up

front with your physician. Either the fee can be cut, or treatment can be arranged through a clinic. Your doctor is your best resource for locating the best possible alternative at a lower cost—far better to ask him or her than to go out on your own.

OVERCOMING "DOCTOR PHOBIA"

Whether the topic of discussion is financial or physical, you and your doctor must speak the same language for any effective communication to take place. Many doctors talk primarily with other doctors, so a lot of jargon gets bandied about. If you don't grasp something he or she tells you, back up and keep inquiring until you're confident that you do. Don't ever feel embarrassed to ask the doctor to elaborate on a point because you think you *should* have caught it the first time.

"Doctor phobia" is widespread, and it may help you to get a sense of the source of this affliction. Doctors are often viewed as a breed apart, as members of some elite and exclusive club. Most people are aware of the rigors of medical education and that it is very competitive even to land a spot in medical school. Doctors seem to have special knowledge, as well as access to special machines and tools that appear to give them power over the rest of us.

The circumstances under which dealings with doctors take place are another source of "doctor phobia." You're stripped down to your underthings—or less—but the doctor is fully dressed. That alone tends to make one feel vulnerable. Depending on the stage of your pregnancy, you might also feel bloated or misshapen. You're in a stark, bright, not terribly comfortable room. You may have to wait—in fact, the question is often not *do* you have to wait, but how long? The roomful of nervous-looking women poring over magazines only serves to remind you of just how important this person you're about to see is. Your doctor is probably busy, as doctors are generally busy, and you may feel stressed by that time pressure. Beyond all this, you're undoubtedly anxious about your pregnancy and feel that this doctor has a great deal of control over your fate.

It's important to get over doctor intimidation. A free exchange of information back and forth is especially critical about caesareans because a doctor's judgment and the mother's participation play a large role both in how the delivery proceeds and how the mother perceives it.

Rather than annoying your physician, your asking questions will probably please him or her. Some doctors are unprepared to deal with today's informed and interested new mothers, but most doctors prefer patients who are knowledgeable and who take an active role in their health and childbirth plans. It's a lonely job to take care of a body whose owner shows no respect for it.

Any question that goes unasked also goes unanswered. It's not always the doctor's fault that the patient doesn't know something. It's up to you to state your concerns and raise any issues you want addressed: how a medication might affect labor or the unborn child, how soon you'll be able to breast-feed. Your doctor should be happy to help you understand important aspects of your delivery because that could make for fewer *mis*understandings and other problems down the line.

Nor should you hesitate to state your wish for a

second opinion. Some women regard this as a sticky point because it may suggest to their doctor that they're questioning his or her competence. But every doctor should accept—if not welcome—a request for a second opinion. The issue is not whose feelings you hurt but the level of care that you get. Many hospitals encourage and even require a concurring opinion for a caesarean. Lots of cases are not clear-cut, and many doctors prefer to hear from an independent source. An attending physician who has been with a laboring mother for hours during a difficult delivery will likely welcome a doctor new to the situation, who might have a clearer perspective on what action is needed.

If you are planning a caesarean, you can choose a doctor to provide a second opinion. Your insurance company may have a list of physicians available for consultation, or a nearby hospital may have an appropriate doctor—say, a department chairman or high-risk specialist—depending on the circumstances.

If the question of a caesarean arises when you're already in labor at the hospital, you may be limited in whom you can get. There would be a consultation with a doctor who's already there, perhaps attending to another patient, or a member of the hospital staff. Ask your physician ahead of time about how the system works at your hospital.

This book has emphasized that the more knowledge you have about your pregnancy and about caesareans, the better. It's a good idea to take notes when speaking with your doctor. This will probably enhance your concentration and keep you from letting any details slip away from you. There's no need to feel silly or self-conscious about doing this—after all, your doctor is probably taking notes to enter into your medical history too.

FINDING SUPPORT AND INFORMATION

If you're planning to have a caesarean or have recently emerged from one, you need not feel alone. Talk to friends and other women who have been through it. Every woman's experience may be different, but everyone's experience is valid, and you're likely to learn a great deal from others. Simply knowing that you're not alone can be comforting and reassuring, especially if medical monitoring and postpartum fatigue have made you feel cut off from others—at a time when you long to feel the closest.

Nor should your husband or partner be excluded from the process. First of all, he is certainly going to be affected by whatever affects you. Perhaps most important, he is more than an uninterested party here. The birth will be an emotionally exhausting, exhilarating, overpowering event for him as well, and his feelings about the caesarean may be every bit as baffling. He may, for example, feel that he let you down, that had he been more supportive or more protective or more aggressive with the hospital staff, you wouldn't have had to go through it. He may be worried about your health and recovery and view you as more fragile as a result. He may feel that the baby is more delicate and requires special handling. He will be most supportive to you and most comfortable with himself if he understands what it is you're facing and exactly what you need from him.

Ideally, your family and friends should also provide valuable encouragement. But not everyone is knowledgeable about caesareans, and they may not be as sensitive as you'd like. Some people may regard a caesarean as the "easy way out" (how wrong they are!) and subtly imply that you chickened out. Some may suggest that your birth experience was diminished. The best thing to do is to ignore their comments and base your judgment on what you know to be true.

Beyond your own private circle, support groups can provide you with help and information. Find one by checking through women's organizations or health organizations in your community. Some organizations that either sponsor support groups or may be able to refer you to one include:

American College of Obstetricians and Gynecologists (ACOG)
   409 12th Street SW
   Washington, D.C. 20024–2188
   (202) 638–5577

American Society of Psycho-Prophylaxis in Obstetrics (ASPO)
   1411 K Street NW
   Washington, DC 20005
   (703) 549–2226

Cesarean Prevention Movement
   P.O. Box 152
   Syracuse, NY 13210
   (315) 424–1942

C-Sec, Inc.
   22 Forest Road
   Framingham, MA 01701
   (508) 877–8266

Council for Cesarean Awareness
   5708 S.W. 69th Ave.

Miami, FL 33143
(305) 666–7090

International Childbirth Education Association (ICEA)
P.O. Box 20048
Minneapolis, MN 55420
(612) 854–8660

National Association of Parents and Professionals for
Safe Alternatives in Childbirth (NAPSAC)
Route 1, Box 646
Marble Hill, MO 63764–9726
(314) 238–2010

Planned Parenthood
380 Second Avenue
New York, NY 10010
(212) 777–2002

APPENDIX A

For Further Reading

Cohen, Nancy Wainer, and Lois J. Estner. *Silent Knife: Caesarean Prevention and Vaginal Birth after Caesarean* (Granby, Mass.: Bergin and Garvey, 1983).

Ehrenreich, Barbara, and Dierdre English. *For Her Own Good: One Hundred Fifty Years of Experts' Advice to Women* (New York: Doubleday, 1979).

Hausknecht, Richard, and Joan Rattner Heilman. *Having a Caesarean Baby: The Mother's Complete Guide for a Safe and Happy Caesarean Childbirth Experience*, rev. ed. (New York: Dutton, 1983).

Inlander, Charles, et al. *Medicine on Trial: Medical Mistakes and Incompetence in the Practice of Medicine Today* (Englewood Cliffs, N.J.: Prentice-Hall, 1988).

Jones, Carl. *Birth Without Surgery: A Guide to Preventing Unnecessary Caesareans* (New York: Dodd, Mead, 1988).

Keyser, Herbert H. *Women Under the Knife* (New York: Warner Books, 1986).

Martin, Emily, ed. *The Woman in the Body: A Cultural Analysis of Reproduction* (Boston: Beacon Press, 1987).

Norwood, Christopher. *How to Avoid a Caesarean Section,* (New York: Simon and Schuster, 1985).

Rich, Adrienne. *Of Woman Born: Motherhood as Experience and Institution,* 10th anniv. ed. (New York: Norton, 1986).

Stage, Sarah. *Female Complaints* (New York: Norton, 1979).

Weideger, Paula. *History's Mistress* (New York: Penguin, 1986).

APPENDIX B

The Pregnant Patient's Bill of Rights

American parents are becoming increasingly aware that well-intentioned health professionals do not always have scientific data to support common American obstetrical practices and that many of these practices are carried out primarily because they are part of medical and hospital tradition. In the last forty years many artificial practices have been introduced which have changed childbirth from a physiological event to a very complicated medical procedure in which all kinds of drugs are used and procedures carried out, sometimes unnecessarily, and many of them potentially damaging for the baby and even for the mother. A growing body of research makes it alarmingly clear that every aspect of traditional American hospital care during labor and delivery must now be questioned as to its possible effect on the future well-being of both the obstetric patient and her unborn child.

One in every 35 children born in the United States

today will eventually be diagnosed as retarded; in 75% of these cases there is no familial or genetic predisposing factor. One in every 10 to 17 children has been found to have some form of brain dysfunction or learning disability requiring special treatment. Such statistics are not confined to the lower socio-economic group but cut across all segments of American society.

New concerns are being raised by childbearing women because no one knows what degree of oxygen depletion, head compression, or traction by forceps the unborn or newborn infant can tolerate before that child sustains permanent brain damage or dysfunction. The recent findings regarding the cancer-related drug diethylstilbestrol have alerted the public to the fact that neither the approval of a drug by the U.S. Food and Drug Administration nor the fact that a drug is prescribed by a physician serves as a guarantee that a drug or medication is safe for the mother or her unborn child. In fact, the American Academy of Pediatrics' Committee on Drugs has recently stated that there is no drug, whether prescription or over-the-counter remedy, which has been proven safe for the unborn child.

The Pregnant Patient has the right to participate in decisions involving her well-being and that of her unborn child, unless there is a clearcut medical emergency that prevents her participation. In addition to the rights set forth in the American Hospital Association's "Patient's Bill of Rights," (which has also been adopted by the New York City Department of Health) the Pregnant Patient, because she represents TWO patients rather than one, should be recognized as having the additional rights listed below.

1. *The Pregnant Patient has the right*, prior to the administration of any drug or procedure, to be informed by the health professional caring for her of any potential direct or indirect effects, risks or hazards to herself or her unborn or newborn infant which may result from the use of a drug or procedure prescribed for or administered to her during pregnancy, labor, birth or lactation.

2. *The Pregnant Patient has the right*, prior to the proposed therapy, to be informed, not only of the benefits, risks and hazards of the proposed therapy but also of known alternative therapies, such as available childbirth education classes which could help to prepare the Pregnant Patient physically and mentally to cope with the discomfort or stress of pregnancy and the experience of childbirth, thereby reducing or eliminating her need for drugs and obstetric intervention. She should be offered such information early in her pregnancy in order that she may make a reasoned decision.

3. *The Pregnant Patient has the right*, prior to the administration of any drug, to be informed by the health professional who is prescribing or administering the drug to her that any drug which she receives during pregnancy, labor and birth, no matter how or when the drug is taken or administered, may adversely affect her unborn baby, directly or indirectly, and that there is no drug or chemical which has been proven safe for the unborn child.

4. *The Pregnant Patient has the right,* if Cesarean birth is anticipated, to be informed prior to the administration of any drug, and preferably prior to her hospitalization, that minimizing her and, in turn, her baby's intake of nonessential pre-operative medicine will benefit her baby.

5. *The Pregnant Patient has the right,* prior to the administration of a drug or procedure, to be informed of the areas of uncertainty if there is NO properly controlled follow-up research which has established the safety of the drug or procedure with regard to its direct and/or indirect effects on the physiological, mental and neurological development of the child exposed, via the mother, to the drug or procedure during pregnancy, labor, birth or lactation—(this would apply to virtually all drugs and the vast majority of obstetric procedures).

6. *The Pregnant Patient has the right,* prior to the administration of any drug, to be informed of the brand name and generic name of the drug in order that she may advise the health professional of any past adverse reaction to the drug.

7. *The Pregnant Patient has the right* to determine for herself, without pressure from her attendant, whether she will accept the risks inherent in the proposed therapy or refuse a drug or procedure.

8. *The Pregnant Patient has the right* to know the name and qualifications of the individual administering a medication or procedure to her during labor or birth.

9. *The Pregnant Patient has the right* to be informed, prior to the administration of any procedure, whether that procedure is being administered to her for her or her baby's benefit (medically indicated) or as an elective procedure (for convenience, teaching purposes or research).

10. *The Pregnant Patient has the right* to be accompanied during the stress of labor and birth by someone she cares for, and to whom she looks for emotional comfort and encouragement.

11. *The Pregnant Patient has the right* after appropriate medical consultation to choose a position for labor and for birth which is least stressful to her baby and to herself.

12. *The Obstetric Patient has the right* to have her baby cared for at her bedside if her baby is normal, and to feed her baby according to her baby's needs rather than according to the hospital regimen.

13. *The Obstetric Patient has the right* to be informed in writing of the name of the person who actually delivered her baby and the professional qualifications of that person. This information should also be on the birth certificate.

14. *The Obstetric Patient has the right* to be informed if there is any known or indicated aspect of her or her baby's care or condition which may cause her or her baby later difficulty or problems.

15. *The Obstetric Patient has the right* to have her and her baby's hospital medical records com-

plete, accurate and legible and to have their records, including Nurses' Notes, retained by the hospital until the child reaches at least the age of majority, or, alternatively, to have the records offered to her before they are destroyed.

16. *The Obstetric Patient*, both during and after her hospital stay, has the right to have access to her complete hospital medical records, including Nurses' Notes, and to receive a copy upon payment of a reasonable fee and without incurring the expense of retaining an attorney.

It is the obstetric patient and her baby, not the health professional, who must sustain any trauma or injury resulting from the use of a drug or obstetric procedure. The observation of the rights listed above will not only permit the obstetric patient to participate in the decisions involving her and her baby's health care, but will help to protect the health professional and the hospital against litigation arising from resentment or misunderstanding on the part of the mother.

Prepared by Doris Haire, ICEA President 1970–72, ICEA Consultant 1982–83.

APPENDIX C

The Pregnant Patient's Responsibilities

In addition to understanding her rights the Pregnant Patient should also understand that she too has certain responsibilities. The Pregnant Patient's responsibilities include the following:

1. The Pregnant Patient is responsible for learning about the physical and psychological process of labor, birth and postpartum recovery. The better informed expectant parents are the better they will be able to participate in decisions concerning the planning of their care.

2. The Pregnant Patient is responsible for learning what comprises good prenatal and intranatal care and for making an effort to obtain the best care possible.

3. Expectant parents are responsible for knowing about those hospital policies and regulations which will affect their birth and postpartum experience.

4. The Pregnant Patient is responsible for arranging for a companion or support person (husband, mother, sister, friend, etc.) who will share in her plans for birth and who will accompany her during her labor and birth experience.

5. The Pregnant Patient is responsible for making her preferences known clearly to the health professionals involved in her case in a courteous and cooperative manner and for making mutually agreed-upon arrangements regarding maternity care alternatives with her physician and hospital in advance of labor.

6. Expectant parents are responsible for listening to their chosen physician or midwife with an open mind, just as they expect him or her to listen openly to them.

7. Once they have agreed to a course of health care, expectant parents are responsible, to the best of their ability, for seeing that the program is carried out in consultation with others with whom they have made the agreement.

8. The Pregnant Patient is responsible for obtaining information in advance regarding the approximate cost of her obstetric and hospital care.

9. The Pregnant Patient who intends to change her physician or hospital is responsible for notifying all concerned, well in advance of the birth if possible, and for informing both of her reasons for changing.

10. In all their interactions with medical and nursing personnel, the expectant parents should

behave towards those caring for them with the same respect and consideration they themselves would like.

11. During the mother's hospital stay the mother is responsible for learning about her and her baby's continuing care after discharge from the hospital.

12. After birth, the parents should put into writing constructive comments and feelings of satisfaction and/or dissatisfaction with the care (nursing, medical and personal) they received. Good service to families in the future will be facilitated by those parents who take the time and responsibility to write letters expressing their feelings about the maternity care they received.

All the previous statements assume a normal birth and postpartum experience. Expectant parents should realize that, if complications develop in their cases, there will be an increased need to trust the expertise of the physician and hospital staff they have chosen. However, if problems occur, the childbearing woman still retains her responsibility for making informed decisions about her care or treatment and that of her baby. If she is incapable of assuming that responsibility because of her physical condition, her previously authorized companion or support person should assume responsibility for making informed decisions on her behalf.

Prepared by Members of ICEA

Published by International Childbirth Education Association, Inc.
P.O. Box 20048, Minneapolis, Minnesota 55420 U.S.A.

Index

Dell Medical Library

☐ 20629-4 **LEARNING TO LIVE WITH CHRONIC FATIGUE SYNDROME**
Edmund Blair Bolles $3.50

☐ 20597-2 **LEARNING TO LIVE WITH CHRONIC IBS**
Norra Tannenhaus..................................$3.50

☐ 20596-4 **RELIEF FROM CHRONIC ARTHRITIS**
Helene MacLean $3.50

☐ 20571-9 **RELIEF FROM CHRONIC BACKACHE**
Edmund Blair Bolles $3.50

☐ 20570-0 **RELIEF FROM CHRONIC HEADACHE**
Antonia Van Der Meer $3.50

☐ 20628-6 **RELIEF FROM CHRONIC TMJ PAIN**
Antonia Van Der Meer $3.50